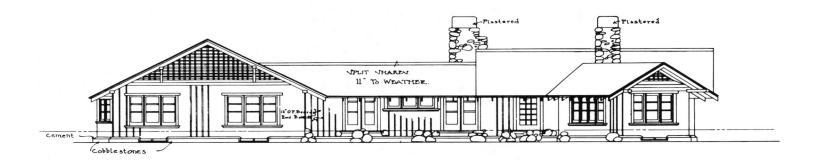

Plastered

Plastered

SPLIT SHAKES.
11" TO WEATHER.

Cement

Cobblestones

GREENE & GREENE

Architects in the Residential Style

GREENE & GREENE
Architects in the Residential Style

Photographs by
William R. Current

Text by
Karen Current

AMON CARTER MUSEUM OF WESTERN ART, FORT WORTH

International Standard Book Number 0-88360-005-6
Library of Congress Catalog Card Number 74-76989

Editorial preparation and design: Morgan & Morgan
Composition and printing: Morgan Press

Printed in the United States of America

Thus it may be seen that in a work of art as in a piece of tapestry, the same thread runs through the web, but goes to make up different figures. The idea is deeply theosophic, one life, many manifestations; hence, inevitably, echoes, resemblances—consonance.

Charles S. Greene

Amon Carter Museum of Western Art Board of Trustees

The Amon Carter Museum was established in 1961 under the will of the late Amon G. Carter for the study and documentation of westering North America. The program of the Museum, expressed in publications, exhibitions, and permanent collections, reflects many aspects of American culture, both historic and contemporary.

This publication and the exhibition which it accompanies have been assisted through a grant from the GRAHAM FOUNDATION FOR ADVANCED STUDIES IN THE FINE ARTS, Chicago, Illinois.

Participating Institutions

ART MUSEUM OF SOUTH TEXAS
Corpus Christie, Texas

UTAH MUSEUM OF FINE ARTS
University of Utah
Salt Lake City, Utah

WALKER ART CENTER
Minneapolis, Minnesota

SAN FRANCISCO MUSEUM OF ART
San Francisco, California

THE ART INSITUTE OF CHICAGO
Chicago, Illinois

BAXTER ART GALLERY
California Institute of Technology
Pasadena, California

Contents

Acknowledgments

Preface

Introduction

DOMESTIC ARCHITECTURE

    The Period as an Epoch   1

METAMORPHOSIS OF A STYLE

    Seeds of California Domestic Architecture   6

    The California Bungalow   10

THE RESIDENTIAL STYLE

    Bases of the Residential Style   32

    The Outstanding Commissions   43

THE GAMBLE HOUSE   69

EPILOGUE   113

Acknowledgments

The photographer would like to express his appreciation to the National Endowment for the Arts for their award of an individual grant to continue this work, and to the Graham Foundation for their support in designing the museum presentation. Sincerest thanks go to Mr. Adolf K. Placzek, Avery Librarian, Columbia University, for his interest and cooperation in allowing photographs to be made of original Greene & Greene plans and drawings, and to Mr. Kenneth Cardwell, Curator, Architectural Documents, University of California at Berkeley.

To the owners of Greene & Greene houses and furniture who opened their homes for this study, the photographer is deeply grateful: Mr. and Mrs. James Richardson, Mr. and Mrs. Raoul Savoie, Mr. and Mrs. Max Hill, Mr. and Mrs. W. K. Dunn, Mr. and Mrs. Alexander Whittle, Mr. and Mrs. Kinzie Miller, Mr. and Mrs. Daniel James, Mr. and Mrs. Harley Culbert, Mr. and Mrs. Edward Remund, Mr. and Mrs. Mortimer Fleishhacker, Jr., Mr. and Mrs. Richard Anderson, the City of Pasadena, and the University of Southern California.

The children of Charles Greene—T. Gordon Greene, Mrs. Anne Roberts, and Patrickson Greene —were of great help and provided valuable insights. Mr. Marcel Sedletzky, architect, encouraged this study at a much-needed time.

Much credit is due Mr. Mitchell A. Wilder, whose enthusiasm, personal drive and professionalism realized this as a traveling photographic exhibition and publication. Finally, to innumerable friends who supported and appreciated this study at crucial moments, both the photographer and the author feel deeply indebted.

Preface

Inevitably the question arises as to one's involvement and interest in a subject. My involvement in Greene & Greene began, really, as pre-knowledge which stemmed from my childhood, for I was a second generation Pasadenan and was raised in a Craftsman home by my grandparents.

I left Pasadena as a young man, returning in the early fifties to visit many of the Greene & Greene houses with student friends who were interested in architectural design. The subject remained, however, in the too-near past. At that point my own values were not yet assured enough to recognize the excellence of my own heritage.

In the years that followed, I turned to the Southwest, seeking origins both in nature and architecture. I became interested in the indigenous architecture of the prehistoric Indian, the subject of my book, *Pueblo Architecture of the Southwest*. Throughout those years, I was drawn toward Oriental art and philosophy, and I had the advantage of knowing some of the best photographers. Paul Outerbridge taught me design, and contemporary photographer-friends Brett Weston and Wynn Bullock taught me, through the practice of their art, that photography is a way of life.

Finally, I returned to my place of origin to perceive and come to terms with that which I had carried within for a long time.

Pasadena   William R. Current
March, 1974

The houses treated in this book are described as they appeared in their most fully-realized states. However, some have not survived, and others have undergone substantial changes. The current state of each is noted in the picture captions.

Introduction

It is long ago and a world away from the two brothers Greene, who worked at architecture as true craftsmen, touching almost physically all of the elements that they brought together to make a house; bringing it naturally into being without noisy surprises, but only the appreciative gratification of those fortunate enough to be able to live there.

Their artistry matured and developed into an influence that went beyond Pasadena and California to become a national style that for its time marked a significant trend. But it is the work of their own doing that celebrates the simple, beautiful modesty of their very special importance.

These are houses where nothing is abrupt; everything that connects, embraces; structure flows naturally from one element to another and joins to become an eloquent part of what comes next.

There is shaded elegance, at once innocent and enormously sophisticated. These houses are true familiars—with an instant and compelling recognition. One remembers them as always there, perhaps momentarily put aside, but never quite forgotten—warm, strong, and glowing.

And so, to these quiet, engaging, lovingly-talented men, this quiet, beautiful book.

Chicago   John Entenza
April, 1974

DOMESTIC ARCHITECTURE
The Period as an Epoch

Architecture is inextricably bound to the whole of man's civilized environment and much of what we know of past civilizations is through their architectural forms. Architecture can provide clues to the prevailing conditions of the age that brought it about—the economic prosperity, the social climate, the technological advances, even the "natural" problems that had to be solved. It stands long after the conditions of the contract were made for its life and tells civilization what progress it has made in becoming aware of itself. Whatever the conditions of birth, its life continues, revealing without comment the limitations and potentialities that wrought its existence, until it transcends the moment of origin, mindless of the social class that paid for it and the style which made it fashionably correct. Then its particular character becomes apparent, for it is also the physical symbol of an artistic expression.

In America, a land where people are noted for their mobility upward as well as westward, perhaps the most personal and consistent symbol of cultural aspiration from the Revolution till World War I is the single family dwelling. The detached house becomes the daybook that reveals, beyond style categorizations and periods, what was uppermost in the American mind—the aspiration sheltered in thought, what one wished to house in his life, the accomplishments he believed he had made. Curiously, it is only within the last two centuries that architectural history has concerned itself with the habitat of the rural or the urban dweller, having left that subject to anthropology. In America the discussion is in the foundling stages even while bulldozers seek to eradicate remembrance of its existence.

The monumental and grand have consumed the interest of those who read the architectural past, yet one of the most unique and significant Anglo-American developments in architecture with no precedent in antiquity was the development of the detached house—the Residential Style of building and living. Arising from a nondescript cottage origin, the detached house surrounded by a private garden developed into a style of middle-class residence that was neither rural nor urban, claiming sanction in both town and country. It settled in carefully planned intimacy with natural settings and it was conceived not only because the new national prosperity from industrialization created the possibilty to own a piece of land and a home, but because industrialization wrought the necessity to escape its own by-products and the problems of a world grown to frightful complexity.

Andrew Jackson Downing, architect and horticulturalist, inheritor of the English tradition of landscape gardening, was the first influential writer on the single family dwelling; his numerous books provided the impetus for future development of the residence. *Cottage Residences,* published in 1842, became the textbook of the American carpenter-builder. While Downing himself preferred the Gothic style of building, his general principles regarding the detached home with a private garden exerted a wide influence on residential building.

In Downing's philosophy the single family dwelling ranked as one of society's best assets, for he believed that from the solitude and freedom of the rural home, genius and character could be directly traced and, in direct communion with nature, the family developed individuality and moral fiber. A home in the best sense fostered a sensitivity to the arts and exerted a moral influence; ideally, it symbolized the elevated ideas of man's life, the highest in emotions, the appreciation of intelligence and the enjoyment of a cultured social life.

Fifty years later the homes of the architects Charles and Henry Greene embodied Downing's principles in what was to be the dusk of the residential style's light. Their houses were the last architectural expression in a tradition that had been nurtured in America—a sense of freedom and pride in standing alone.

As homes conceived and nurtured in the last of this tradition of freedom, their residences bespeak gentility and purpose, with the individual expressed but self-controlled; as artistic expression, the work of the Greenes proclaims excellence and transcends the meaning of its time. Coming to terms with their work is worthy of our reflection, for although they built in the twilight of an epoch quite divorced from ours in its tempo and values, they nevertheless expressed the spirit of man aspiring toward perfection and union. Architecture embraced emotional and spiritual realities as well as physical ones, and these creative spirits engendered a personal world for themselves by making a home a work of art as well as a practical, functional environment for their clients. Into the total experience of creating three-dimensional architecture, the Greene brothers invested all that they knew, all they aspired to, everything they believed about man's innate oneness—and if the client understood nothing of all that, he nevertheless had an extraordinary house, suited to his needs.

The Greene brothers' homes present the most coherent body of work, along with the Chicago School, of any modern architects, and it is at the very least instructive to pursue the development and demise of this phase of residential living.

It was the age of Morris in England, the Impressionists in France, and the eve of inauguration in America of Ulysses S. Grant when the Greene brothers were born. Charles was born in 1868, the same year as another notable artist, Charles Rennie

Makintosh; Henry was born in 1870. Their father was a doctor and evidently the boys enjoyed the security and advantages of a middle-class family. The days must have been paradise for two curious, adventurous boys, seventeen months apart in age, who were invited to their grandfather's farm in Rhode Island every summer. Both Henry and Charles sustained throughout their lives an interest in natural things; remembrances of their grandchildren reveal long walks with grandfather Hal who could tell them the generic names of plants, sea life and flowers, and of Charles who could weave marvelous tales.

In the 1880s, Charles and Henry together attended the Manual Training High School operated by Washington University in St. Louis. To Mr. Woodward, the mentor of the first progressive program, manual training meant more than simply vocational training or the learning of craft; he gave it liberal arts status. He taught manual training as a means to synthesize the abstractions of the mind and the concrete abilities of the hand. It was a new concept of teaching manual skills as a means of visualizing abstract principles, and there was less emphasis on the practical objects of outcome than on the principles learned. Equally instructive was the experience of materials themselves, revealing to sensitive minds and hands intrinsic qualities and strengths. The Greene brothers later gathered an entourage of skilled millmen, wood carvers, stone cutters and other craftsmen whom they taught to execute details as they designed them. They themselves hand-worked and finished the inlay of furniture; they even hand-shaped the larger beams of some of their houses—details conceived in their fertile imaginations, their skilled hands could execute.

The professional architect had made his debut on the American scene with the first architectural degree, granted in 1863. But even more recently had architecture truly become the business of architects when the Greene brothers began their studies at the Massachusetts Institute of Technology. A classical education was proffered alongside Richardson's Trinity Church in Boston, built in 1859, from which internationalists reckoned the birthdate of American architecture. Whatever the alchemic proportions, Charles and Henry later transmuted the academic and the Richardsonian influences into their own original formula.

Boston's social climate also yielded some of its secrets to Charles and Henry through the influence of a socially-prominent aunt. The young men experienced the manner of living of the privileged and discovered the social requirements of those in position, no insignificant aid when later creating a home for wealthy clients. Upon graduation the brothers went to work for firms of size and reputation. It was a comparatively brief interlude—two years—until the establishment of their own office in Pasadena, far removed from the sources of their architectural mentors, but not their influence. Traveling in 1893 to visit their parents in the West, the brothers carried the unsynthesized elements of an architecture, according to a contemporary architect, of "the most perfect houses that have ever been built."

Pasadena, already an established winter resort and mecca for the retired, was the home of Dr. and Mrs. Greene, who had taken residence there for Mrs. Greene's health. It also was becoming one of the select residential areas in America. Charles and Henry sensed the mystique of the land protected by the magic mountain, softened by rolling hills and orchards, and nourished by a stream through a wooded arroyo. What began as a holiday ended in a commitment by the brothers to stay in Pasadena and declare their talents.

The architectural office of Greene & Greene (two men scarcely twenty-five years of age) opened in 1894. With what confidence and belief must such an act have been invested, yet they possessed the surety of their abilities, well-learned and practiced, and the American spirit of freedom and independence, born of a revolution. They were the inheritors of the 19th century's lively and inventive architectural symbols of American man freeing himself of the box. From myriad sources evolved the Greene brothers' rich architectural vocabulary and the synthesis of a unique architectural expression. To understand the work of these two men, it is necessary to briefly retrace these sources and to look at the 19th century, when America metamorphosed from agrarian to urban society.

Colonial builders in the early days of domestic building had bestowed two essential elements upon American architecture: a flexible ground plan which could be expanded as need and economics indicated, and the plain wall, which brought all elements together into a balanced and unified whole. In particular, they developed the clapboard wall which dominated wooden building and of which many of the diverse "styles" or periods in architectural measurements have been variations.

A nail and a stick, two of the products of industrial progress, conjure up no great image of innovation or revolution. Yet, in combination, they led the American vernacular into a new realm. With the machine-made nail and saw-milled lumber, the balloon frame came into being.

At the same time, Andrew Jackson Downing published his pattern book, which pictured the board used as vertical member rather than horizontal clapboard. Coupled with the balloon-frame technique, which seized upon the skeletal energy of framing sticks placed vertically, the builder, pattern book in hand, developed the board-and-batten style. This became a significant phase in the evolution of the single-family residence. It was a new organic architecture, rooted in the craft of the carpenter-builder and concerned with the needs and customs of the American way of life. In skilled technique rather than grand styles lay the creative process and, from 1840 to 1870, the builder-as-architect brought into being domestic American forms.

By 1870, America, burdened with the woes of industrialism and a world grown too complex, began to seek a purer, more understandable way of life. People glanced back with nostalgia to the sea, perhaps to rediscover their origins and to return to the place where a simpler way of life expressed itself. By the mid-seventies, the professional architect emerged to a place of prominence in America. While he acclaimed what had been the freely-conceived development of a thoroughly American architecture, his academic training began looking to other sources of inspiration. In this mood the Philadelphia Exposition honoring the Centennial, opened in May of 1876. Seen in the light of a nostalgic yearning for a return to the simple past, the colonial style buildings on display seemed to fill the hunger.

At the same time, several Queen Anne style buildings, representing the English return to the vernacular, captured the wish of the people for an ordered, more abstract architectural symbol of security and roots in the past. What resulted was a brief if curious marriage between the Colonial and Queen Anne styles, producing a new domestic architecture, based upon carpenter-builder techniques and expression, but extended by the artistic training of the architect.

Many excellent houses derived their inspiration from the Queen Anne style and colonial enthusiasms, but among those who advanced the new architecture one significant step further is William Ralph Emerson of Boston. He created the first all-shingled house, elucidating the mass of a continuous surface. To the plain colonial wall, which European architects were ever trying to embellish with one style of decoration and then another, he applied natural, indigenous materials, shingles; the stick-style skeleton was clothed in stained and textured materials like a feathered bird. This evolution involved a new sense of the qualities of space and light in three dimensions and it paralleled the two-dimensional developments on canvas by the Impressionists in Europe. Aesthetically, the surface suggested order rather than ornament.

With this legacy and that of the early American flexible and informal ground plan, Henry Hobson Richardson, designated the grandfather of American architecture, carried the evolution of the shingle style one step further. He created the open, interior space as a unified whole—rooms flowed from the spatial nucleus, the central living hall, and the interior volume became a continuous space which could be adapted to a variety of functions and expression. In Richardson, the synthesis was complete; the American house was its own invention, an original style that sensitively adapted itself to the American dream. The home had become open and free-flowing to express man's desire to break out of his boxed life; materials were expressive of his desire to return to the earth and be rooted in a place; requirements were simplified and more informal, a reflection of a simpler life. If the shingle style seemed more primitive, it was, nevertheless, a reflection of the American's newly desired way of life. This style had assimilated many influences and then gone beyond to become a thoroughly American architectural style. Strictly American were a new sense of ordered yet free space, a simplification of space and surface, and an interweaving of interior-exterior forms. Middle-class America spread its wings and shouted freedom in its architectural spaces, even as the gilded age, in pompous mimicry of past glories, raised monuments of palatial size.

Amidst all this, bearers of other cultural messages arrived on American shores, among them Oscar Wilde. He brought the gospel of the Aesthetic Movement whose message at that moment infused every art form in England. Aesthetics—defined as the science of the beautiful or the philosophy of taste—became the prime concern, and the thrust of the movement in England was education of the layman. Once a group of cultivated persons defined and decided on matters of taste, the near-bankrupt domestic arts would be revitalized. Oscar Wilde became a serious proponent for the cause and, in 1882, decided upon a trip to America to elevate the taste of the uncultured. To his reported surprise, the other side of the Atlantic contained a populace versed in the Aesthetic Movement through books and reprints, and most probably through Gilbert & Sullivan's *Patience,* a play which lampooned the movement. On the whole, the Americans proved better educated than their English cousins. Crowds thronged to his lectures and complete press coverage followed his travels. Wilde captured the imagination of a widely diverse audience with his unorthodox ideas of "Art for Art's sake," and "the secret of Life is Art." He pointed out the wealth of native materials available for domestic arts in America. His influence must have been enormous for the tour lasted 18 months by demand, a truly personal triumph for Wilde as well as for the spirit of the movement. By the 1890s there were more than thirty organizations devoted to a revival of the arts and crafts, if somewhat on the margin of society.

Other cultural influences were also making an imprint, most notably the Japanese. In England, much of the impetus of the Aesthetic Movement came from the new forms and thought brought by Perry on his return from the first major Western intrusion into Japan in over a hundred years. The Impressionist painters in France likewise reflected the influence, as such paintings as Monet's portrait of Zola in 1868 reveal.

In America the Japanese influence spoke most fluently in three-dimensional terms, in architecture. At the Philadelphia Exposition, already noted for the sensation the Colonial and Queen Anne contributions created, an important, if subtler effect was exerted by Japanese architecture. Workmen arrived from Japan one year before the opening to erect two structures. What began as amused curiosity in the project ended in open admiration for the straightforward design and planning, the honest construction, and the almost total absence of decoration, except for wood carving. Such was the interest that the new American architectural trend absorbed and used many of the Japanese elements. Large firms such as McKim, Mead and White copied the Japanese method of framing room volumes, and of using small recesses and interwoven moldings and screens. More importantly, the simplicity and honesty of the Japanese structures touched a sympathetic nerve in American feeling and contributed to developments of the 1880s in an inspired rather than eclectic manner.

In 1885 the first book on Japanese architecture appeared, done by Edward Morse who had traveled extensively throughout Japan, sketching and making diary entries. His picture of the exterior of the Japanese house showed it resting on stones pounded into the earth, unassuming and unsubstantial in appearance. The roof created the major interest; there the Japanese invested great variety of form and structure in their inventive use of shingles, tiles or thatch. Temple roofs exhibited particularly imposing forms with their grand upward sweep and gables, and their deep eaves, sometimes carved, providing shade. Two or more walls were of sliding screens covered with paper, a fact over which Americans had marvelled in Philadelphia in 1876.

As for environmental experience, once one entered from the dust and noise of street life, he found himself enchanted by an aura of country life, serene and contemplative, for the artistic face of the Japanese home presented itself to the garden, and the largest and best rooms opened onto a garden veranda. The interior proclaimed the craftsman's honest construction and careful attention to the selection and preparation of materials—grains and colors matched, and irregularities were exploited for their rustic quality. Morse noted that suspended ceilings revealed neither nail nor peg holes. If decoration existed, it was exquisite carving, according to Morse. Cross-beams of Japanese homes had no trusses or braces as did some of the uprights, but decorative use of bracing was often applied.

Morse's domestic architectural study, reprinted in book form numerous times, was not the only sphere of his influence. Under his aegis, several other Americans took residence in or extended trips to Japan. Ernest Fenollosa, lecturer in philosophy from 1878 to 1886 at the University of Tokyo, admonished by Morse to gather the last impressions of indigenous art before it became totally westernized, gathered a vast collection of Japanese art. He became an authority on the subject, re-establishing it in the Japanese school system and, at the same time, bestowing upon the Boston Museum of Fine Arts one of the finest collections in the world. In 1892, he returned to Boston, the home of the two recently-graduated Greenes, to deliver much-publicized lectures on Chinese and Japanese literature and arts.

Fenollosa appeared the following year at the Chicago Exposition, where the Japanese had constructed three pavilions, each of a distinct period in Japanese architecture. They symbolized 1,000 years of design and development. The buildings appeared all the more remarkable and elegant in their human scale amidst the pomposity and monumentality of neo-classic buildings, which cleverly disguised the progressive and forward-looking demonstrations of industry and science housed within. Imaginatively designed in the form of the legendary Phoenix bird, the structures on the wooded lagoon appeared to hover over the lake. As form and symbol, the grouping was praised as the first entirely original, indigenous Japanese building seen in this country. Charles and Henry Greene numbered among the thousands that saw the structures.

If the academic finery of the Chicago Exposition buildings seemed gossamer poison to the spirit of Sullivan and Richardson, nevertheless for many the gilded creations and affectations of the past embodied the aspirations for a national greatness and the values that a newly rich nation could afford to display. For these people, the "Victorian" fantasies exhibited the wealth, exuberance and pride of the individual who could build an empire and proclaim his success.

Thus, cheek by jowl there existed two spirits, both reliant upon the abundant resources of a rich industrial nation and both believing in the control and possession of nature: to one, richness meant mountains of imported objects and gilded furnishings; to the other, it meant objects made by American artisans and designers. To the first, the grandeur of past styles born of older cultures symbolized the values they sought. By comparison, to the second the value of a home lay in its response to the American way of life, created by the native genius of local architects.

In that decade before the turn of the century, Europe experienced the same dichotomy of the academician versus the rebel, but there the artistic rebel movement paralleled the political, social and moral upheavals.

Over 100 art periodicals appeared in the decade before the turn of the century, born of that division of spirit. Determined to break with academicism and to come to terms with modern industrial life, Art Nouveau emerged in Europe like the full-blown Minerva. A wealth of national variations all reflected the same desire, the renewal of art in life. The language form, whether in applied art or architecture, was equilibrized yet restless movement, best recognized by the undulating whiplash line. In search of beauty artists turned to nature for design inspiration and seductively translated her infinite variety into individualistic architectural and decorative expression. In Brussels there were Victor Horta and van de Velde; in France, Guimard and Lalique;

Charles Rennie Makintosh in Glasgow; and their American counterpart, Louis Comfort Tiffany.

Tiffany began to move away from the large ecclesiastical work in stained glass and thought in terms of applying his art to creation of lamps and glass-metal objects during that decade of ferment. He foresaw a new surge of art for the people in creating useful objects for daily life. Tiffany perceived a new kind of patron in the more-educated masses; they were less prejudiced and tradition-bound, "unsophisticated," and therefore willing to accept new forms. In realizing that objects of daily use touched a wider audience, he saw that the artist could educate in the truest sense through the creation of beautiful, utilitarian forms. And, unlike William Morris, he believed in the machine as the work-horse of an art industry. It made viable the production of vast quantities of art objects for a rapidly-expanding complex society. On the other hand, industrialization bound men more irrevocably to the machine and the resulting squalor, ugliness and debased mode of life for the average American at the turn of the century offered little evidence in praise of industry.

Among the many attempts to counter the encroaching industrialization were those of Gustav Stickley and Edward Bok. Stickley sought to counteract the spreading malaise of giantism and the artlessness of machine production in two ways. He started his own manufacturing firm and began to produce simple, craftsman-like furniture, ". . . comfortable, well-made and fine in structure, proportion, workmanship and finish." He used woods of native origin almost entirely, his favorite being oak. Secondly, he encouraged the already existing craftsmen to take pride in their work and calling. Stickley saw a nation choking itself to death with luxuries and accoutrements contrived for a thousand artificial requirements and he perceived a people intensely commercial, fond of the good things of life, proud of their ability to "get there," carrying the country to its demise—that in 1907! Stickley held out hope for the pioneer spirit to prevail over the passion for money-making and extravagance, and began to propound the arts and crafts as the building blocks of a total environment. He became editor of the *Craftsman Magazine* and the acknowledged leader and official spokesman of the Craftsman Movement, if it can be called such, for it remained peripheral to and small within the mainstream of production.

Stickley dedicated the first issue of the *Craftsman Magazine* in 1901 to the expression of

Morrisonian principles, both artistic and socialistic, in making art a means of realizing life rather than something apart from it. Toward that end, Stickley published in following issues such writers as Tolstoi and Morris on social philosophy, articles on Art Nouveau and the decorative arts, and the work of new leaders in house design and town planning, Voysey and Sullivan among them. Pervading the pages was the underlying belief that the artistic lay not in the eccentric or unusual but in common materials made beautiful. Simplify forms, materials, and decoration was the message of the diverse articles given space in the magazine. Stickley based his appeal on the eighteenth-century notion that natural man possessed both power and goodness, and that he had the will to overcome the debased machine-made world, as the motto, "Als ik kan," or "if I can," indicates. But the heart of the movement shifted, and soon depended upon the middle class who were the only ones able to afford the products.

On the architectural front appeared Edward Bok, editor of the *Ladies Home Journal,* who resolved to "make the world a better or more beautiful place to live in," having been appalled by the wretchedness and inadequacy of housing for the working American. Bok admittedly knew little about architecture, art or decoration, but he must be numbered among the more progressive men of the day. He sought to involve the architectural profession in the design of moderately-priced houses—from $1,000 to $5,000—and in 1897 he published the first in a series of articles on "Model Homes of Moderate Cost," including plans and specifications. He approached Frank Lloyd Wright to do two designs for *Journal* readers, which appeared in 1901. But what was to influence Bok's readers (Wright's advanced concepts and designs reportedly brought him no commissions whatever) was an architectural development in California called the "bungalow."

All the elements for a new architecture presented themselves. California basked in an abundance of fine materials which found sympathetic treatment in the hands of numbers of skilled people. There were European craftsmen and Yankee shipfitters who took pride in their work. The European immigration had brought trained servants as well, knowledgeable in the art of running households. Another shore had yielded the sensibility and expertise of Japanese gardeners, so that a special group of immigrants existed in that atmosphere. Then came a unique group of settlers, educated and bred in the values of the Anglo-American eastern seaboard, of moderate but easily sufficient means who had shed their eastern habitats and patterns of living along with their heavy winter clothes. They thought of a comfortable home as an extension of themselves rather than as an investment.

California had proffered itself to an unusual and independent growth of indigenous styles—first the missions, then the territorial style and the Spanish hacienda—and it supported the simple, single-family dwellings that the carpenter-builder had provided in response to the large influx of western settlers. Passive in comparison to the harsh climates of the East, the landscape presented a picturesque display of rolling hills, orchards and vineyards, suitable for any style, imposing few limitations in its gentleness.

Into that promising milieu moved many fine architects, trained in the East, ready to launch their careers. Though eclectic in approach, they were still imbued with the spirit of individual expression—Richardson's contribution to the status of architect as artistic leader. As a whole, these early 20th-century western architects and the Chicago School picked up where the East left off. Their work constituted the last two original strains of residential architecture and they appeared nearly simultaneously: the prairie style in the Midwest and the bungalow in California.

Defined by an historian of the California architectural frontier as an unconscious synthesis of the entire panoply of 19th-century California domestic architecture, the bungalow seemed to answer multifarious housing needs. A prolific number of articles and descriptions of bungalows began to appear. They became a regularly featured item in the *Ladies Home Journal* from 1904 onward through the decade, and the *Craftsman Magazine* praised the "good, simple straightforward houses" of California as closer to the craftsman ideal than any other. Gustav Stickley himself believed the bungalow to be the most "genuine expression of American domestic architecture that has yet appeared." As a style, the bungalow was hard to place. Some credited the Japanese house as the progenitor, others suggested that the bungalow was more closely akin to the hacienda or patio house, while still others depicted the bungalow as founded upon the Mission style or, strangely, as an offspring of the Indian house which was in fact a British colonial implantation that served as a rest house along main roads of travel.

What was at the heart of this last evolution, whatever influences or styles an architect might assimilate and whatever the economic means of the client, was the creation of a total environment and a manner of living—honest, unpretentious yet gracious, where exterior, interior, furnishings and setting blended together. A bungalow was neither to present an austere front nor to create a sense of status for the owner. A shelter, not from other men but from the forces of nature, ideally it provided a congenial atmosphere of tamed nature which might be contemplated. The bungalow symbolized a setting of informality for enjoying a harmonious family life, while providing the atmosphere for genteel, more cultivated pastimes; comfort rather than luxury, and quality in lieu of ostentatious display. For the 20th-century man, health and the regenerative power of sun and pure air were virtues, and beauty in utility meant Truth.

Onto the stage to create one of the final expressions of the American vernacular in domestic building stepped the Greene brothers. The bequest of the Yankee builder, puritan ethics of integrity and clear-cut values, and the accomplishments of benefactors such as Richardson had all played their part. To that moment the Greenes brought a genius for design, an innate feeling for materials, and a rich architectural vocabulary, derived from numerous forms and influences. They were artists whose medium of expression was architecture; if that architecture created an environment in which gentleness and higher-minded values could flourish, it was an important but lesser goal than the goal of art itself. The total experience of exercising and realizing all that they knew and possessed innately—that was the stuff of their creation. They built a personal world for themselves—inspired and self-styled—through the evolution of three-dimensional architectural concepts, as did Sullivan and Wright.

When the curtain fell in the mid-teens of the century for the firm of Greene & Greene, the causes were part of a much larger pattern. More than the loss of a clientele or the onset of war was the loss of heart of the American people. Gone the rebellious spirit, born of a revolution, and in its place, conforming Babbittry grown unwilling or unable to listen to the prophets who demanded a redirection of American life away from object-mindedness and material security.

The Residential Style was in its twilight, portending the demise of an epoch. Americans retreated to their caged boxes, which could be built row upon row in a seemingly unending stream, and expressing, for all their mass power, a sadly imprisoned state.

METAMORPHOSIS OF A STYLE
Seeds of California Domestic Architecture

The San Gabriel valley, where the seed of the future City of Pasadena still lay fallow, had dozed through the gold rush, tranquil and relatively undisturbed, along with most of Southern California. With the completion of the transcontinental railroad in 1869 and the frontier made easily accessible, the valley woke from its slumber with a jolt. In 1873 a group of prospectors from Indiana arrived in the San Gabriel valley seeking different treasure. They found their "gold mine"— a gentle climate and beautiful land conducive to good health. A year later, the nucleus of what was to become the City of Pasadena began to take shape as Indiana colonists arrived. An early settler of Pasadena remarked that "even the most sanguine mind among us pictured nothing in the future beyond a quiet little hamlet made up of pleasant, health-giving homes surrounded with fruits and flowers and affording a safe retreat from the great busy world." A mere twenty years proved that vision naive; the treasure, once discovered, could not be kept seclusive.

In the 1800s, Southern California's climate and terrain smiled benignly upon groups of immigrants from New England and the Midwest, populating Los Angeles and other communities. But when, in 1887, the Santa Fe Railroad reached the Pacific Coast and subsequently received a ten-million acre land subsidy, the beginning of a land boom resounded on the frontier. Luring would-be Westerners with such inducements as $1.00 railway tickets from Kansas City to Los Angeles, the railroad hoped to promote the settlement of their vast acreage. Golden communities such as Santa Monica, existing for the moment only in the fertile imagination of the railway developers, were glowingly advertised in terms of the "Zenith City of the Sunset Sea." Clearly, the quiescence was over. Thousands of people, attracted by the prospects of this undeveloped land

where snow rarely fell and fierce cold never pervaded, boarded the train with hopes and household goods securely in tow. Within a year, however, the imagined mecca turned into mirage—the Zenith City was in reality a desert, as were other advertised communities and, in 1888, the land boom crashed nearly as suddenly as it had rocketed.

With the demise of promised opportunities, already-established communities found their populations reduced to less than half their rush-day number. Pasadena's origin, however, had been rooted in more fertile ground than simply the minds of developers; and while the real estate crash left the local citizenry shaken, they nevertheless determined that they would control their city's destiny from that time on. Local society resolved to return to the principle upon which the city had originally been founded—the creation of a residential community, with tourism the primary industry, and horticulture a secondary interest. A local citizen summed up, "We of Pasadena are consumers, not producers;" and Pasadenans relinquished, almost gratefully, any pretensions as a city of commerce and industry.

To have stated such a goal—that of being a select residential community—would have been presumptuous had Pasadena been a Dodge City or a boom town of mining days. But Pasadena had been a city in the making before the onslaught of developers. Architecturally, it put forth the same wooden face as did the established communities of America, exhibiting a legacy of residential styles as well as an Opera House and two fine resort hotels. The immigrants who had been the builders and shapers of the domestic vernacular—the traditional frame cottage with clapboards—had brought with them their cultural past and their carpenter skills; they became the shapers too of Southern California's

domestic homes. They contributed but slight regional variations and pattern-book stylizations to an essentially American wooden theme. Even though the temperate clime and physical gentility of the landscape could have embraced many styles, the domestic residences of the 1880s were assortments of wooden boxes, models of previous knowledge and experience, which confined spaces in a formal, closed life style.

In truth, both the carpenter and the stuff of his craft—wood—were imports to the semi-arid land. Only technology and enterprise made wood easily available and relatively inexpensive, for redwood and pine grow only in northern California and fir in Oregon. Wood became "indigenous" by the entrepreneurial maneuverings of such men as Henry Meiggs in Mendocino and William Carson in Eureka, who quickly assessed the need for housing the thousands of new inhabitants.

With the balloon-frame technique, the result of the technology of the sawmill and the nail machine, such cities as San Franicsco and Chicago had been spawned practically overnight. While neither so sudden nor dramatic, Southern California's architectural birth also evolved from that same technique, which had transformed carpentry from a very old craft involving slow and meticulous methods of joinery, to a more nearly mechanized skill. Thin 2″ x 4″ studs on plates rising the entire height of the building could replace heavy timbers, and a few nails held the light sticks firm without violating the strength and durability of timber, as did mortises, tenons and cuts for joints. To the skeleton frame the carpenter could apply the products of the sawmill—either ship-lap or tongue-in-groove boards, or shingle siding—eliminating hand-fashioned sidings. The rapidity with which this technique could be applied by less-than-master craftsmen dictated the style of domestic architecture throughout the country, and Southern California's frontier was no exception. Carpenter-built homes were the norm; they have proved sturdy and neat even though skeleton frames seem daringly thin and hollow wall construction defies structural appearances. In fact, passage of time has proven them incredibly worthy, but time-bound senses tend to disbelieve. Visually the early vernacular houses elicit little feeling of primeval forces—of gravity and thrust in tension—but rather seem earth-bound and static, as if they had been dropped into place rather than fitted into the land. Houses themselves usually accomplished the "settling in" with some sag and warp as a result. Carpenters invariably painted their houses white, be they clapboard or vertical board-and-batten, and capped them with hipped roofs, high-pitched forms that prairie winds and New England snows naturally dictated. Residential areas spoke of crisp Yankee neatness and, in the 1880s, Pasadena's countenance bespoke its Eastern and Midwestern lineage.

With this legacy, Pasadena already could boast a residential section of some note. When the land boom ended, there was an additional spur to her residential claim, for many talented architects had been among those attracted west by the promise of cities to be built. Now they settled in more established communities, Pasadena among them. With the influx of Eastern architects came the so-called Queen Anne style. Actually, it comprised a curious mixture of forms with little resemblance to the actual architecture of Queen Anne's reign; the style, in Montgomery Schuyler's acidic words, "sucked the dregs of the whole English Renaissance." The aspiration to create some sort of liaison between free composition and classic detail evolved into a multitude of forms which defied clear definition, but which could readily be adapted to any size requirement or pocketbook. Perhaps more important than the stylistic variations which the Queen brought to domestic architecture was the psychology which motivated acceptance of the style, the psychology of a new bourgeois, urban culture, experiencing second and third generation riches. With the emergence of these *nouveaux riches* in' the East came the concern over culture and "good taste," an unknown term before the Victorian era and a somewhat degenerate offspring of the Aesthetic Movement's cultivation of the beautiful. Gentility and refinement became very American concerns; it was felt that with the renaissance of classical details some link with former values might

be asserted, but even more deeply-rooted was the hope for a renaissance of previous American values. Queen Anne, dressed in her classical appliqués, conjured up a picturesque past that had seemed full of promise and certainty, and it was touted as a style of "freedom, charm and coziness," which gives as delightfully vague an idea of its substance as its appeal. Thus, the immigrant architect brought the Queen, both in form and philosophy, to Southern California's already existing vernacular themes that clients enthusiastically chose from pattern books for carpenters to copy. Californians indulged themselves in even more exotic forms which had no historical precedent in their culture, place or land.

California also had fostered a native architecture, that of Spanish origin. It was being rediscovered and re-evaluated as California's true colonial heritage about the time of the Greene brothers' arrival. Just as the Philadelphia Exhibition of 1876 had created nostalgia and a yearning for a simpler past which had turned the Easterners back to their colonial architecture, so were their western cousins now seeking *their* colonial heritage. A. Page Brown, an architect, introduced the western legacy of Colonial architecture in a Mission style building at the Chicago Exposition in 1893, a structure admired and acclaimed. Locally, Californians began promoting "Mission Style" as their true heritage. But the primitive if charming adobe architecture, which been built by Indian hands with only simple building skills, hardly adapted itself to 20th-century urban requirements. Spacious, elongated horizontals of thick-walled, dark-interior adobe, yawning and stretching upon abundant land, proved inflexible and impractical for urban living. To mold forms originally rooted in Franciscan religious traditions in Spain and since mutated on Mexican soil whence the *padres* came, in most cases proved futile for even the most talented architects. Clearly domestic and industrial needs in a worldly society did not conform to mission styles. Unfortunately, in the one area in which logical adaptation of the Mission style might have been successful—church architecture—forms never materialized. Gothic remained synonymous with Church in the American mind. Perhaps more important, adobe, a time-consuming material to make and to construct, proved undependable against cracking and leakage; walls were necessarily two to three feet thick and even then unsubstantial. As source rather than form of inspiration, however, the Mission style was of primary importance to many

architects, including Charles Greene. He admired the work of these early shapers of California art and most of all the spirit of the men who had created the missions. He wrote of them:

The old art of California—that of the mission fathers—is old enough to be romantic and mysterious enough, too. Study it and you will find a deeper meaning than books tell of or sundried bricks and plaster show. . . . The same spirit that made it possible for so much may again produce something as good. We of California are not pessimistic. In truth and love these men believed that they were doing God's will. No wonder that the work they have left is beautiful. Simple as it is, and rude, it has something that money cannot buy or skill conciliate. It runs in every line, turns in every arch and hangs like an incense in dim cathedral light. This little band of men, so full of inspiration, so sure of success, could not fail—they did not fail.

Still in search of a colonial heritage, architects turned to the Spanish adobe hacienda of the early Land Grant days. That "heritage" proved more a romantic hope than a reality, for the few remaining examples of the early adobes were homes made by pastoral people with few building skills, using only the materials at hand. Surviving early adobe houses were crude and humble affairs at best. Literary descriptions of the grand haciendas, such as that in *Ramona,* were in fact far from accurate, for the typical ranch adobe stood one story, had earthen floors and mud sills. Thus, attempts to discover California's architectural soul among adobe forms proved a dead-end trail, although adaptations of some elements found their way into what truly became California's unique style. What did result, with somewhat more success, from the search for a past, was a revival of various Mediterranean styles, such as the Italianate and Morisco, but these remained peripheral to the quest for a regional style which truly reflected California. During this architectural ferment, Charles and Henry Greene came to the West.

When the great Chicago architect, Louis Sullivan, described his arrival by train into Chicago in 1873, at age 17, he wrote:

The train neared the city; it broke into the city; it plowed its way through miles of shanties disheartening and dirty gray. It reached its terminal at an open shed. Louis tramped the platform, stopped, looked toward the city, ruins about him; looked at the sky; and as one alone, stamped

his foot, raised his hand and cried in full voice:
'THIS IS THE PLACE FOR ME!'
He walked through the streets of Chicago: "Louis thought it all magnificent and wild: A crude extravaganza: An intoxicating rawness: A sense of big things to be done."

For the Greene brothers, both in their early twenties, arriving by train in Pasadena twenty years later, the scene could not have been more antithetical to Sullivan's Chicago. In contrast to the shanties of Chicago, there stood a residential community with neat, painted homes; in direct opposition to the crude extravaganza that Chicago presented, Pasadena was characterized by gentility and a slow-paced, well-bred reasonableness. Resort hotels were fed by an increasing stream of visitors and the city's prosperity rested comfortably on the steady rise of tourism, rather than the tough-minded generosity of plutocrats making fortunes. In direct contradiction to "ruins about him [Sullivan]," stood the beauty of the Crown of the Valley about the Greenes. It is not certain if Charles and Henry Greene intended to explore the possibility of establishing their own practice in Pasadena, but with the entire country—and more crucially the Eastern seaboard—in the throes of a a financial crisis in 1893, it is not improbable. Their decision to do so was a bit less immediate and bombastic than Sullivan's; witness Charles' statement on the matter in comparison to Louis':

The wondrous climate, freedom of life and the lure to try the new are so tempting that even when one comes with a host of traditions one is apt to find it 'so different' that one hesitates—and at last stops to listen, most often to be convinced.
Sullivan had committed his talent to the "big things to be done;" the Greene brothers entrusted their architectural fortune to a land which Indians had first claimed as home.

Before the first whisperings of a city were heard in the peaceful valley, Pasadena had been a chosen dwelling place of Indians. They had lived on the banks of the arroyo in the 1770s, surrounded and protected by high places and fed by a rushing stream of life-giving water. Below them, the Arroyo Seco yielded game of all sorts, including grizzly bear, wildcats and mountain lions. And under watchful Indian eyes the semi-arid land was coaxed to relinquish staple crops. Historically, places of beauty have been sought by Indians, who feel the mystique of the land and who live close to the magic of natural forces; even in 1890, though subject to "civilization," the beauty of the infinite varieties of

scenery surrounding Pasadena gave many cause, "for the first time to look upon the great 'out-of-doors' long enough to think about it . . . learn to love it." Nestled in a valley surrounded by high mountains—the San Rafael Hills to the west and the San Gabriel Mountains to the north, dominated by sometimes-snow-blessed Mt. Wilson—Pasadena still evoked a sense of magic. To the west, from cupolas and higher buildings, lay a view of the Pacific and, from the San Pedro shores, Pasadena appeared paradisical with brilliant golden poppies dividing the purple San Gabriel Mountains from the green fields below, wrote Richard Dana in *Two Years Before the Mast.*

To add intoxication to the heady wine of nature's endowment was a superb climate, the original treasure sought and the *raison d'être* for the creation of Pasadena. By the time the Greenes arrived, major journalistic efforts thrived upon waxing more eloquent than any previous article on the wonders of the Southern California climate and, more particularly, that of Pasadena. Writers affirmed, "Nearly always perfect weather conditions prevailed"—perhaps an overstatement in view of occasional torrential rains, floods and earthquakes, but for those surfacing from snow-laden winters of freezing cold, not so far from true; for the health-seeking *emigré,* virtually unquestionable.

If the description of Chicago in the 1890s as a "flat smear, endless drawl of streets and shanties . . . filth in the air and slime underfoot, and dust in the nostrils . . . this foul spot on the smiling prairie, this blotch on the fair face of Nature!" even approaches a reasonable facsimile of reality, it is small wonder that Pasadena seemed particularly alluring to people from the Midwest and East. And the added attraction of reasonably-priced property either for winter residence or all-year homes, now that real estate speculation was under control, created a thriving and relatively stable haven amidst the shipwreck of many of the country's financial centers. The future character of Pasadena as a nonindustrial, "bedroom" community seemed further assured by the San Gabriel Valley Railroad's connection to Los Angeles which provided the possibility for professional men to work in the city.

Charles and Henry Greene, already familiar with society in Boston, found Pasadena similarly social-minded. Local society in Pasadena, however, while basing its standards on rather conservative Eastern models and emulating the Victorian affectations of the Anglo-American seaboard, had evolved more from the informal friendships and mutual in-

terest clubs of the early settlers than from family background. Consolidation of ranks by those who had nurtured Pasadena from village to town happened after the real-estate fiasco and its attendant intrusion of outsiders. Circles had tightened; those who had come but 20 years later were separated as though by a chasm from the "natives." Society drew impenetrable boundaries, becoming more exclusive and ingrown as the '90s progressed.

An article which appeared in a Los Angeles publication in 1895 described more closely, perhaps, the aspiration of Pasadena society than the reality of its bases, for Pasadena possessed no Bloomsbury group, neither did it boast a studied representation of New York "blue-book" families. Local society did spell its name in capital letters, however, and it was a very real force in Pasadena's life.

A correspondent of a St. Louis paper has evidently been making a violent study of social life in Southern California, says the Pasadena News, and comes to the conclusion that Pasadena is the only place in Southern California where 'society' as it is known in the East exists and flourishes. Moreover, we are told that Pasadena has had an aristocratic and ultra-exclusive social life founded on eastern models for ten years. In Los Angeles, says this wrecker of eastern ideas, it is 'political or business influence and money that gives one the open sesame to society, but in Pasadena it is brains, culture, family and previous standing in the East only, which admits one to the close intimacy of select circles. One might,' says the critic, 'live in Pasadena ten years and not meet the exclusive people that make up its real social life, unless they had letters to some of them, but in Los Angeles the building of a big house and a little rattling of coin, and the doors open.' Whatever their credentials, local society took the city's destiny firmly in control and affirmed that Pasadena should secure its position as a residential area without equal in Southern California. As one writer put it, "Pasadena asks no better name than that of the City of Homes."

The strangely mysterious landscape of sea and magic mountain, rushing stream and semi-arid foliage; seductive climate of dry Santana winds, cool ocean draughts, desert-like heat of summer and mild winter; "the sun-warmed ether near the blush of roses"—these sang a Circean song and the brothers decided to remain.

Charles and Henry opened the office of Greene & Greene in 1894, and launched their career in designing domestic housing. Their early work, predominantly in current, eclectic styles such as the Queen Anne and Neo-Colonial, reveals a sure hand and competent eye, judged by classic tradition and training. These houses assuredly placed the brothers among the talented architects of the times, although not distinguishing them.

In 1897, Frances Swann employed the Greenes to design a substantial home. Mediterranean revivals, an off-shoot from the less-successful attempt at Mission adaptations, provided new grist for the architectural mill, and the Greene brothers also turned their eyes southward. For the Swanns they produced a gracious home which bears the influence of the Italian villa, particularly in the interior with its vaulted, painted ceilings and deeply-carved woodwork. In fact, Charles' interest in the Italianate style proved more than flirtation, for when he and his new bride honeymooned in 1901, traveling first to England, Mrs. Greene's home, and then to Italy, Alice Greene later told her son that once in Italy she rarely saw her new husband: he headed daily to the architectural library near the Spanish Steps to scan the vast collections of drawings and architectural renderings. The Italian experience never left Charles; it suffused much of his thinking and emerged architecturally much later, transformed by years of his own practice and experience.

More immediate and direct an influence was the Italian concept of a home with as much importance attached to the surrounding grounds as to the house. Home was delineated by the horizon rather than four walls. This idea transformed much of their later design where the home was conceived as part of a well-balanced domain which included house, garden, terrace, patio and open porch, affirming its birthplace in its relationship to the land and embracing the landscape as its decoration.

The entire body of the brothers' early work expressed a coherent, competent classical vocabulary, but it did not foretell the aesthetic vision which lay only a promise, even as the caterpillar carries within his lumbering body the secret of its butterfly potential. Their vision metamorphosed slowly, testing and probing within the cocoon of classical architectural forms until the moment of full-blown emergence, when the unmistakably unique and beauteous forms found their wings. But that was several years hence; in the meantime, the situation as the *fin de siècle* years approached and America faced the new century was a determinant of California's future as well.

The prospect of the 20th century inspired reflections and comparisons upon the past hundred years, and speculations as to what the next one hundred might have in trust. While history is a stream, with ebbs and flows, with the past ever-present, blending into the future, the turn of a century cannot help but become a symbolic ending-beginning; who among us has not felt the urge for "resolution" at the end of one year and the beginning of another?

The 19th century had been heir to unbelievable changes and extraordinary progress by anyone's reckoning, and all signs pointed to an even brighter twentieth century, if leaders of technological advances could be believed. On the domestic front, however, optimism found little fertile soil. For if industrial barons seemed to be making giant strides, it was at the expense of rural America.

Architecturally, urban, domestic habitats appalled and assaulted the senses, as the Dutch immigrant Edward Bok discovered. He realized that architects had little or nothing to do with housing the middle class in urban America and he resolved, as editor of the *Ladies Home Journal,* to try to do something about the situation. He sought out prominent architects, asking them to design moderately-priced houses in a variety of styles, with the idea of publishing the plans and specifications. Predictably, the response on the part of the architectural profession was less than enthusiastic, architects feeling, on the whole, that they were being excluded from the money-making aspects of designing and supervising a home. But as public response to the *Journal's* offering rocketed circulation to over one million, most capitulated.

Though of horse-and-buggy vintage, the homes which Bok presented stand, from the aspects of convenience and comfort, as the precursor of the modern house. Standard household equipment—improved plumbing, electricity, gas ranges and central heating—made possible by the same industrial gains that also enslaved, were available to more people than before dreamed of. Hygiene was "in" at long last, and standardized fixtures for both the bathroom and the kitchen, *sans* servant, were available. In design, styles ranged from Colonial variations—a plan by Cram appeared in 1896 and a Dutch colonial design by Bruce Price—to country houses in the English manner.

In 1897, the first of the *Journal's* "Model Homes of Moderate Cost," with plans and specifications, appeared. In that same year views of interiors, some from Pasadena homes, materialized on the printed page as well as an article on the Rose Parade. By 1899, Pasadena houses had been counted among the "Prettiest Country Homes in America." In the 1901 February issue, "A Home in a Prairie Town" appeared, and in July "A Small House with Lots of Room in It," both designed by Frank Lloyd Wright. The latter home was priced at $5,835. These houses were designed for the middle class, the general readership of the *Ladies Home Journal.* Wright himself expressed the belief that, "Democracy needed something basically better than the box to live and work in . . . so I started to destroy the box as a building." Ironically, the people comprising that democracy did not respond to the offerings of such talented architects, and Bok's earnest campaign to upgrade the level of the average American's domestic menage resulted in general mediocrity, judged from the standpoint that no progressive developments in domestic architecture resulted.

Nor did the *Journal* stimulate significant departures in the area of furniture. In 1900, designs of Charles Rennie Makintosh, the Scotsman who figured among the avant-garde in modern design, were published. Following those, Bok commissioned the American, Will H. Bradley, who had achieved international recognition for his graphic creations in the *art nouveau* vein, to design some model interiors and furnishings exclusively for his magazine. Sadly, the richly-toned color schemes that Bradley drew appeared in black and white. Most of his work never materialized beyond the printed page, as *art nouveau* styles only really became popular in the graphic arts in America.

American readership responded somewhat enthusiastically to other editorial suggestions, however, particularly in interior decoration, and here the *Journal* proved to be more influential. Secretly, the readers may have sighed with relief that the love affair with mistress Europe, in all her ormolued, gilded, curvaceous trappings was declared officially over. A rash of articles entitled, "Good Taste and Bad Taste in . . ." appeared, comparing everything from houses to pillows considered in good taste to those obviously out of vogue. Settings and furniture of another period and costume moved to the debit side of the ledger, replaced by simple materials for furnishings and furniture. Floors shed their heavy carpeting and windows their weighty coverings. Unassuming interior room settings were featured and, in 1902, a simple dining room done by Greene & Greene appeared alongside designs by Frank Lloyd Wright and Myron Hunt.

METAMORPHOSIS OF A STYLE
The California Bungalow

What was to exert the greatest influence upon the domestic architecture of the country was the development of the California bungalow. Essentially, bungalow origins sprang from the entire range of California's domestic shelters—which consisted of one transplant upon another, brought in memory or pattern book from previous habitats and built with previously developed methods. Synthesis involved neither the creation nor invention of any single architect; nor was it a conscious response to the strangely new environment in which architects found themselves. Neither was it the result of every community being "new" and therefore open to new and progressive ideas, the bizarre and unusual. Communities consisted of immigrants, the least radical force in cultural change, and tradition was as vital a part of their carpenter's kits as the tools within. More broadly, the history of architecture is the ledger of one cultural debt after another owed to previous cultures and civilizations, and America, including the West, knew few innovators. Architects continued to ransack the past for inspiration and, "In the year Nineteen Hundred," wrote Charles Greene, "Southern California had scarcely awakened architecturally to the possibilities offered by its climate and topography. The natural beauties of its hills and valleys, its mountains and dry rocks, its rugged live oaks and chaparral, its flowers, its weeds, its brown earth and sandy washes . . . it made good reading. It awakened the interest of the tourist; but the architects of domestic work had already learned their lesson at school or in the office."

The development of the bungalow emerged in response to a call for suburban housing by a variety of people seeking a respectable place in the sun at a reasonable cost. The California bungalow evolved as the regional answer for the sun-worshippers, the health seekers, those grown old and now searching for warmth and respite from the rigors of cold winter habitations, and the lovers of nature. People sought a new life where environment dictated fewer absolutes, but they necessarily required forms which previous culture and training had taught them constituted home. Thus, architects gathered the influences that California had graciously accommodated throughout the 19th century, with varying degrees of success, and produced the state's first truly suburban vernacular, the bungalow. It remains with the prairie style house as the last phase in the development of the American vernacular domestic architecture.

Beginning with the traditional wood frame model, California's inherited architectural forms began to be rearranged into a style labeled "California Bungalow." In truth it was a series of individual plans with as many types as architects, and the entire range of wooden transplants was incorporated in varying combinations. Simple, rustic board-and-batten cottages of redwood done by carpenters, the shingle style and Queen Anne, brought by architects in the 1880s, comparable wooden styles such as the Swiss and Japanese all contributed to the California Bungalow. Less directly were elements of California's adobe past incorporated. Heritage in the Bengalese house, from which the term bungalow derived, was even claimed, but the nomer appealed more to imagination than the prototype. The bungalow had little in common with the Anglo-Indian version, designed to protect travelers from the burning blaze of heat, and ill-suited to domestic living. The name was in fact more a Victorian affectation that sounded interesting; as Charles Greene remarked, there was little Indian but the name, for "few of us have seen a real one [bungalow] . . . but we cannot shake off the appellation however removed it may be from a semblance of anything Anglo-Indian."

There are nearly as many definitions extant as there are examples of bungalows; stylistically, the bungalow had many guises. Generally, the type prevalent in Southern California could be characterized as a simple home of small size, informal in plan, economically done with only as much stylistic variation as money could afford, and picturesque in setting. Whether of one or two stories, the bungalow was recognized by a long simple roof line, sometimes with a single dormer or windows in the gable. Most prevalent, whatever the stylistic stance, was the unpretentious appearance of the bungalow. Above all, "a bungalow shouldn't attract attention to itself." Materials announced their origin by remaining in their natural color, white wooden facades yielding at last to wood in transparent stains. Redwood or cedar shakes—a long kind of shingle, yet differing from the shingle in its uniform thickness throughout—effected a picturesque image and brought the house into harmony with the soft brownish-green of the mountains. From the landscape strewn with field-stones, builders appropriated nature's markers. Lichen-cloaked, smooth from rubbing together over centuries and made definitive in form, the gray stones metamorphosed into structures of durability and function, even if somewhat overwhelming in smaller structures. Used for piers upon which the foundation rested, chimneys, and sometimes indoors for the fireplace itself, they added a pleasing tone and texture depending upon the skill and use of the builder.

Regardless of the size a bungalow might assume, rooms stretched in a rambling open arrangement (a gift from Queen Anne), deriving a natural openness to each other and to the outdoors; had heating been a requirement for much of the year, it would have been a highly impratical scheme. But the sun shone 300 days out of the year and the treatment was not only picturesque, it allowed more sun. To live *al fresco* as much as possible was now considered important for the healthful life, and any element which would provide the opportunity to be outdoors yet enjoy comfort was incorporated in bungalow design. In some cases, nearly every room had access to an inside court or a view of the garden. Stuffy parlors gave way to living rooms with shelves for books. Casement windows and French doors were used, providing a more direct sense of communication with the outdoors. Wooden construction made them practical, for they could be grouped along a plane of timber rather than cut out like a hole and intruded into a wall. Even the front door provided less sense of enclosure with its solid front dissolved by panes of leaded or art glass.

In the bungalow as in the earliest colonial homes, a fireplace commanded a position of importance. Even though central heating was standard, and the plan of the house was liberated from the fireplace, it remained a dominant structural element in the bungalow. Considering the size of some bungalows, the definition of a home as a "fireplace boxed-in" was not far afield. Nevertheless, the fireplace reigned, much to the mystification of foreigners, who considered it curious that one would enjoy sitting before a fire roasting his feet and face while his backside was exposed to the great draughts of air the fire drew from every crack and crevice. The hearth endured in the American mind as the center of comfort, cheer and good comradeship to man, the fire-gazing animal, and it symbolized the meaning of home, as it still does. Even the modernist, Walter Gropius, when asked why he had included a fireplace in a very modern design, replied, "My psyche demands it." In the craftsman's view the fireplace set the tone for the interior scheme and all other elements deferred to it as the pre-eminent starting point of a well-balanced decor.

Bungalow interiors varied, according to the extent of the builder's or architect's involvement in creating it. Generally a variety of woods prevailed, used both in structure and furnishings; walls were either totally of board-and-battened wood or partially wood, complemented by soft-toned plaster. Bright colors, if conducive to simplicity and consistent with style, were used, but Victorian plush red was definitely *passé*. The presence of good color, stated the *Craftsman Magazine*, "is in itself an incentive to the simple life. From it results that sense of quiet, rest and satisfaction which calms the unwholesome

longing after many things." The *Ladies Home Journal* concurred, often featuring pastel-toned decors, including matched furniture.

Interiors sported a less-than-ambitious collection of furnishings, and appeared almost sparse in comparison with the museum-like domestic interiors of the typical 19th-century home. Stiffly designed formal wall furniture gave way to built-ins: bookcases, cupboards, shelves and nooks. Wicker, reed, rattan and craftsman furniture of sturdy oak supplanted settees and overstuffed styles, and the *Journal* ran a series of articles on making one's own furniture from inexpensive woods such as pine, cedar and hickory. Wooden floors remained commonplace, but depending upon the taste and wealth of the owner, they either lay bare or only area rugs were used. Navajo or domestic hand-woven rugs were a common inexpensive acquisition; oriental rugs also were commonplace, though a bit more expensive. Availing oneself of native, scarcely appreciated materials and designs, and capitalizing on the beauty of simple materials rather than buying ones of ascribed value were encouraged; the trend clearly was to avoid anything that tended toward display. The luxury of "taste" substituted for the luxury of cost as the pacesetters declared that the successful home looked simple.

Compared to the Victorian home harboring galaxies of objects—collections and assemblages of *objects d'art* and fusty curios—the bungalow seemed a poor relative. Objects which related to one's more casual, natural surroundings prevailed, and the hand-made became vogue. Commonly displayed were Rio Grande pottery and Indian baskets, plentiful curios in the Southwest and of good quality; Oriental bric-a-brac of all kinds, such as Chinese ginger and tea jars, lacquer trays and willowware, Japanese vases and hangings; and wares of the arts and crafts practitioners. All found a home in the bungalow. In the more affluent homes, Rookwood pottery, small Tiffany pieces, beaten copper bowls and items from Liberty & Company existed. Simple prints and watercolors of pleasant landscapes done by a member of the family who hobbied as an amateur painter adorned many a wall.

In the January, 1904, issue of the *Ladies Home Journal*, a pictorial article entitled, "The Comfortable Bungalow in California," featured bungalows ranging in price from $3,000 to $5,000 and in size from seven to eight rooms. With this the bungalow made the national scene, and from then until the war years arrived, bungalows were featured regularly in

the magazine. As the 1900s pressed onward toward rising prices and more consumer goods, rafts of variously titled articles on the bungalow—"$1,000 Bungalows . . . $2,000 Bungalows . . . $3,000 Bungalows," "The Easy Housekeeping Bungalow," "The Bungalow Made of Plaster," even "The Bungalow from $250-$2,500" appeared, featuring more and more California bungalows. The *Ladies Home Journal* never sought to actively influence its readership in the stylistic choice of a home, but it did campaign for designs which were "beautiful because they were useful," and panned as strictly bad taste designs with fussy angles, those which impeded light and air, and houses which lacked "quiet purpose" due to meaningless decoration, and especially those houses which sat in total oblivion of the surrounding land. Bungalow designs seemed to avoid many of these evils. Bungalows appeared in such faraway lands as New Zealand, and multiple adaptations on the theme spread throughout the country.

Gustav Stickley, too, began to feature homes in his *Craftsman Magazine*. In his article, "Simplicity and Domestic Life," he synthesized the *Craftsman* idea of a home as the place in which character was fashioned and in which the life of each individual flourished. He expounded the view that if a home's surroundings and influences did not promote a higher degree of mental, moral and spiritual values, particularly in free-thinking persons, then all the efforts to reform society's ills were of no avail. He wrote that not only must the joy of work be restored to the individual, but also that his home must be a place of peace and comfort, closely related to nature, so that his resourceful, high-minded nature would be regenerated.

Stickley's ideas on the necessary components for a *Craftsman* home corresponded to a great degree with those of the bungalow, and he has been credited with turning the middle class toward the bungalow. He advocated large open rooms with quiet nooks for semi-privacy, a fireplace as the center of family life, and an open dining room for more relaxed and friendly entertaining. He suggested simple, comfortable areas for a family's common business and pleasure. Staircases as prominent and beautiful features created a refined relationship between the social life of the family and its private individual life upstairs. Interior colors based upon natural wood tones, soft and mellow, but in harmony with an individual's taste, infused the atmosphere with a serenity from which gentility and reason could emerge. Outside, homes should be of natural textures and colors; the exterior should disappear into the landscape rather than impose itself upon it. While being both economical and practical, the *Craftsman* home, if truly an honest and direct response to individual requirements, would be aesthetically pleasing as well. Above all, it should provide the possibility of a close relationship with the web of life and an intimacy with that primal source of artistic inspiration, Nature.

A later book on bungalows listed such types as, "the Swiss chalet type, the retreat or summer house, the Adirondack lodge (built of logs), the New England Seacoast bungalow (colonial in style), the Chicago (that is, the prairie style), and even 'the house that is not a bungalow though built along bungalow lines.' " Bungalow became a delightfully vague categorization, covering almost any style, but as the new century pressed onward and·the cost of building increased nearly 40% from 1900 to 1907, bungalow, if it implied nothing else, it meant an inexpensive home. A writer on bungalows in the '20s was quoted as facetiously remarking that the bungalow should be defined as a "house that looks as if it had been built for less money than it actually cost."

Bungalow design found fertile soil in California, coming into the supple hands of talented architects who turned their sights toward building for the proletariat as never before. As a result, more and better houses began to appear.

Nowhere was the bungalow's development more remarkable than in Pasadena, described by a frequent contributor of articles on homes and design as "famous for her well-designed artistic small houses." In 1911, a Los Angeles architect declared:

Los Angeles, the whole of Southern California, joins to congratulate the city at the Crown of the Valley, not for a beautiful spot to be found here and there in Pasadena but for that breadth and evenness and ever present charm which she presents to the visitor. This charm is found not alone on her famous boulevards, but up and down each and every little side street, lined as they are with the most picturesque, the most homelike, the most enchanting of residences, the Bungalows of California. After all it is the bungalow of Pasadena which has made the reputation of the Bungalow of California.

Charles and Henry Greene contributed to that reputation. They were less innovators than transformers, taking as their point of departure a low art

form—the bungalow—which in most cases never rose beyond that level. But as the architectural critic, Montgomery Schuyler, wrote, "For architects who love their art and believe in it, the 'point of departure' is much less important than the point of arrival, and by such architects the historical styles of such architecture will be rated according to the help they give in solving the architectural problems of the time."

Synthesis began with the Greenes as the 1900s progressed. They turned their well-trained, eclectic minds to California's architectural heritage and their artistic awareness upon the significant elements of the time and place. They shed their neo-colonial and Queen Anne motifs and began to explore the possibilities of the craftsman-built home. Their vision was fed by the unadorned statements of adobe form and they appreciated the genius of the Mission fathers in their placement of building to site. They plumbed the New England heritage in which they were steeped, and they looked to their own Richardsonian background, seeking synthesis rather than revolution, essence rather than form. They also sought inspiration in foreign architectural styles to which they had long been exposed, beginning to domesticate and naturalize the elements which so often appeared merely as an exotic or picturesque touch. They sought substance instead of decoration.

To their already existing love of nature spoke the Italian and Japanese; both cited by Charles as lovers of the out-of-doors, whence the love of art is conceived. In the Italians' use of the garden as an element of architecture and the Japanese sense of architecture as a concentration and perfection of the hills and trees, the Greenes resolved their own concept of the house. They perceived in the Italians' love of nature the ability to contrive a setting to enjoy it, for as Charles remarked, "Nature does not plant trees where we want them for shade, neither does she place flowers where we may see them when we will." Italian gardens were creations, as much as their fine paintings. The Italians contrived the possibility for man to enjoy nature's romantic aspects as artfully as the Japanese made it possible for him to contemplate nature, regardless of the size of the "natural" space. Between the stark geometry of post and beam and the free and sensuous rhythms of the rock and tree, the Japanese mediated the dichotomy of man in nature and man as nature.

In Japanese architecture, too, the Greenes perceived the evolution of the craftsman's skill and

his innate sense of materials. Unlike the Western philosophy that considered the need for the whole of nature to be subdued and exploited, the Japanese believed wood a sacred material. The essence of the material was rarely violated, and any process which would mar the quality of texture and grain—as did paint and varnish—was considered an artistic crime. Neither was humbleness of function a cause for less than perfection in the forming and fashioning of wood. Therefore, the domestic use of wood for the simplest house was no less an aesthetic exercise than if for a Buddhist temple. While the Yankee craftsman competently constructed clean, crisp homes that would weather harsh winters, his Japanese counterpart built to express spiritual and emotional values. For him, fine workmanship was the mark of his character and an expression of joy for life. Carelessness and cheapness of workmanship resulting in ugliness was an artistic travesty against the gods, not merely against a client who might complain. The aesthete nature of the Greenes was drawn to this use of the common materials, the same as those of Yankee craftsmen, where intrinsic beauty and inherent richness were exploited for themselves.

Chalet architecture had long been a source of imitation for the carpenter-builder. It appealed to his craft as it existed and, perhaps more profoundly, to that secret dream of an idyllic way of life lived happily ever after in a little cottage in a pastoral setting. Derived from primitive, rural mountain shelters, the chalet was folk architecture, picturesque and with every form spawned by a real need. Dana had described the chalet as the "universal building core," but houses all over America acquired only superficial touches of the chalet in the form of detailed carving and decorative elements. Charles and Henry turned to the core of the chalet, which was its profound sense of shelter. The exterior— neat, solid, economical—merely proclaimed what the interior affirmed: no false framework, no hidden construction nor lost space. There was no unnecessary form nor meaningless decoration in chalet construction, which was but another language using post and beam vocabulary.

Essential to the chalet's sense of shelter was the roof. The chalet roof, in comparison with the high-pitched forms of colonial design, presented a solid, lowered profile, neither complicated nor unusual in shape. Beam ends extended beyond the supporting walls and the lengthened roof line provided a short overhang that sheltered rather restrained balconies and outside stairways. The compression of the massive roof seemed to anchor the chalet firmly into its mountainous setting, while the gentleness of its slope made it *simpatico* with its environment. Under that broad brim, wooden walls of dressed red pine and timbers, cloaked only in stain, gave a swarthy, deep-hued complexion to the structure. Beam ends of the interior walls projected through the exterior and were dovetailed and dowelled in undisguised joinery, creating brackets and consoles which supported overhanging balconies. Another dominant aspect of chalet construction was the great stone fireplace, and houses characteristically rested on stone foundations as well. Casement windows, graced with shutters, were used, but the uprights went beyond cross pieces and became patterns of design. Decorative carving was done on structural members only, usually on balconies and shutters, for folk art arises from function and, in the case of shelter, there is little time or resource for additional ornament. Chalets perched themselves in strange and unexpected places in the hope of courting every sunny moment and a view of the valleys. Much of their appeal stemmed from "simplicity and adaptiveness to surroundings outside," two qualities which Charles believed vital to the attractiveness of any wooden house.

Thus, the brothers implanted the seeds of other minds and imaginations, from other times and places, to bring about a new hybrid, neither revolutionary nor trendsetting, not even a pacemaker that would, or could, lead to something new. The germination began as they turned to a low art form, the California Bungalow, and began to house middle-class Americans. Therein begins the flight of that metamorphosed butterfly.

Arturo Bandini, scion of a Spanish family of early California, approached the Greenes and requested a simple Spanish-style house. It was a deceptively simple request, for Bandini was a man assured of his tastes who knew the sort of life style he wanted to pursue. He neither aspired to nor perhaps fully understood Georgian formality, and his home was to be an extension of his personality rather than a suggestion of rank in life. He sought self-expression rather than good taste. It was scarcely a commission architects considered worthy of attention, if they considered doing such a small commission at all, as Edward Bok had discovered. But apparently commissions were slowing down: a financial crisis of 1901 collapsed many money

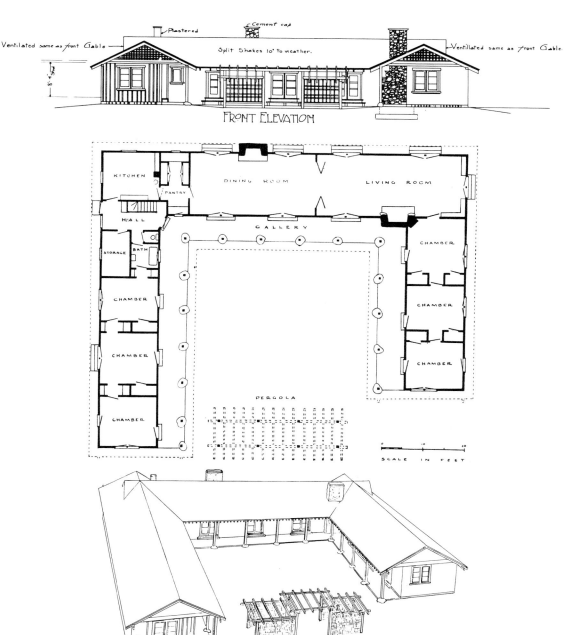

Bandini bungalow, Pasadena, 1903. (House demolished.)

institutions and its effects filtered westward. The Greenes turned every past experience, every talent, every perception toward that commission.

Beginning with the simplest kind of plan, borrowed from the Mexican hacienda where rooms attach to each other and to an inner court, the Greenes opened up the Spanish compound. The living rooms lay across the back of the courtyard, the chambers for the men of the household in the left wing, those for the ladies to the right. The fourth side of the compound the brothers enclosed by architectural use of a pergola to complete the design and lend a sense of privacy even as the Italian Vilino did. Thus the court became more a patio, an architectural element the Greenes began to use in later houses. But the major innovation lay less in their plan adaptation than in the use of materials, for they borrowed the rudiments of the only California house that was not an Eastern simulation, the lowly redwood shack, common throughout the area. Constructed of simple board and batten and left to weather in its natural state, the shack rejected formal values, more because of circumstance than intent. Nevertheless, the shack provided that indirect impetus upon which the Greenes' philosophy began to mold itself. The simple shack sparked their sense of artistry, where cheap and expensive have no meaning; where a material is beautiful because of its intrinsic qualities.

To the Mexican plan of the Bandini home they applied redwood board and batten, consciously leaving it in its natural rough texture and coloration. To the wood they applied, as did the Japanese, a carefully selected stain to preserve the material without marring its substance, leaving nature to her weathering: over the years the pith in the wood slowly wears away so that wood grain stands out clearly and changes its velvety color with the exposure to wind and weather. The interior of the original redwood shack was left in its natural wooden state, again a consequence of lack of money rather than intent. Charles and Henry left the inside of the Bandini house natural redwood but with a difference: they planed both boards and battens to a smoothly textured surface and coated them with a light oil on ceilings and walls.

Fieldstones were gathered from the site, although they were thought by many architects to be a homely material and much too heavy and ugly. With them the brothers displayed a virtuosity of masonry rivaling the best stonework of the shingle-style houses and elevating the stones from rustic

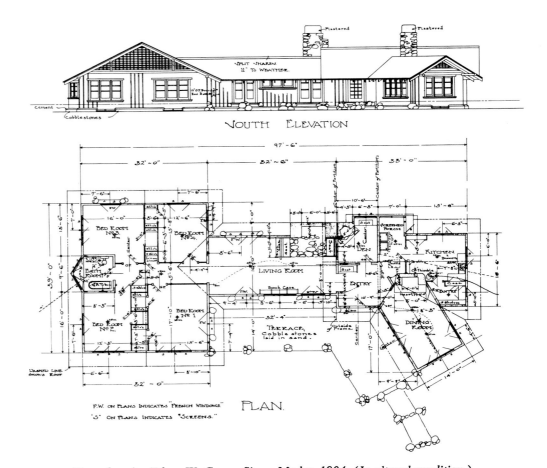

Bungalow for Edgar W. Camp, Sierra Madre, 1904. (In altered condition.)

clumsiness to artistic forms. They used them for chimney and hearth, and rested upon a shelf of the smoothly textured, gray stones, a massive wooden beam for counterbalance of color and texture. They treated them in an unmistakably Japanese fashion, using them as post supports for the beams of the inside galleries of the courtyard, hollowing each rock so that the post rested within it. A simple roof of wooden shingles covered all, pitched to provide ventilation and employing trellis work in much the same manner as the Japanese.

Looking backward from today's vantage point, the Bandini house seems almost commonplace; for its day it truly was not. First, it was conceived with common materials, exploited for their intrinsic qualities, both aesthetic and structural. Now the common transfigured (as well as the exotic extant) became the province of the architect; in accomplish-

ing transformation rather than mere utilization lay the genius of the Greene brothers' craft. It was the common post and beam, with Yankee millwork providing the noun and verb of construction, but unlike the carpenter-builder who applied his trade to a set of given materials, the brothers consciously applied their art, transcending carpentry to make an architectural statement on a shack style. Secondly, the Greenes, as had the Japanese and Swiss, began to explore structure-as-decoration, even as Pugin had admonished the architect years before to "construct decoration—don't decorate construction."

To simplify is never a simple attainment; it takes breadth of experience, confidence and cultivation. The Greenes, now in their thirties, having been practicing architects for ten years, possessed these qualities; more, they possessed the sense of the artist. Now they were ready. The Bandini bungalow became a signpost on the Greene brothers' architectural frontier and even appeared, five years later, in the prestigious magazine, *Studio International,* which claimed it to be the "first of these interesting homes [Southern California Bungalows]."

After the Bandini bungalow, the Greenes designed two other homes in the hacienda vein. The Hollister house in Hollywood, which an early writer described as possessing a delicate feeling of lightness and a true sense of honest construction, was considered a more refined version. Planned for a family with six children, the court became the playground, and Mrs. Hollister could look upon it from any of the ten rooms in the house. Similarly, the Camp house in the Sierra Madre area above Pasadena had the same patio design, but the house conveys more a feeling of the Swiss mountain house to many observers, with the slope of the roofs corresponding almost exactly to the slopes of the Sierra Madre mountains in the background, giving the house a perfect sense of fitting into the landscape.

The single-level Bandini style had the potential of becoming a highly cultivated design, but the trend was not followed, and the Greenes themselves began to design houses of more than one story. The element of economy may have played no small part in this since, as Wright reported, building costs were steadily rising from 1900 to 1907. A one-story house was not inexpensive to build unless one could be contented with a cheap finish and a less stable type of structure, a sacrifice which the Greenes notoriously would never make. With the cost of a building at that time divided between materials and labor at approximately a 2:1 ratio, it became more economical to enclose a second or third story under

a single roof, one of the most expensive elements of a building. For little additional expense, the living area could be increased by twice or three times at less than one-third additional cost, and less land would be appropriated for the house itself, leaving more room for planting.

In 1903, the brothers started to build what was to become a cluster of houses on a piece of land called the Park Place Tract, which bordered a reservoir on one side and the Arroyo Seco to the front. Perched on the edge of the arroyo they created a streetscape referred to as "Little Switzerland." Charles had already chosen this site for his own home in 1901, for he felt that the arroyo was part of that beautiful environment that so blessed Pasadena as few other cities. The Arroyo Seco was a deep gash, beginning in the Sierra Madre mountains to the north, curving its way down and threading the western edge of Pasadena, and ending in the Los Angeles River to the south. A stream bed had carved its way through the arroyo, gushing when thaws came and then full of trout. In the Arroyo Seco Canyon, a wide variety of trees and wildlife flourished and, as late as the 1890s, it was the scene of hunts for game of all sorts, a camping area, and a place for sports contests (the origin of the Tournament of Roses). It remained at that time a luxuriant natural garden of ferns and wild flowers, carved, molded and planted by Nature, and it yet possessed a "woodsy wildness" that Charles Greene loved, where solitude was still possible.

Construction began on a home for three sisters, shouldering Charles'; this was followed by a commission for Judge Willet in 1905, a house for F. W. Hawkes in 1906, and alterations on an already

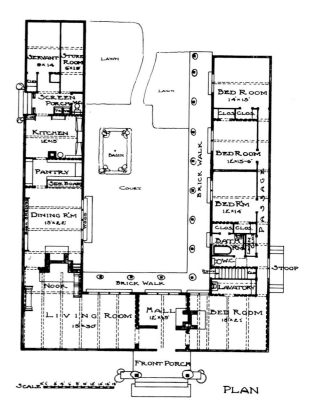

House for Mrs. Cora C. Hollister, Hollywood, 1904. (In altered condition.)
Above: *Plan.*
Below: *Interior details.*

WEST SIDE OF LIVING RM, HALL & BED RM.

existing house, for the Neills. Then a last home in 1907 for Mrs. Ranney completed the tract. Proceeding along the terrace from Charles' house, the brothers had done a house for the Theodore Irwins in 1903, which they subsequently enlarged into a quite prominent home in 1905, and immediately across the street existed an earlier commission, done in 1902 when Charles had returned from Europe, which is more fully described in later text.

Seen individually, each house displays the thoughtful planning, solid construction and balance so characteristic of the architects' homes; as an integrated whole, the tract reveals an ingenious and extraordinary ability to effect that liaison with the surroundings and intimacy with the land that was a particular gift. The whole truly provides an insight into what "tract" housing could mean.

Intimations of the predominant role the roof was to assume in Greene & Greene structures are seen. Spreading lower and sheltering larger areas than its mentor, the chalet, the eaves provided a broad overhang protecting the exterior walls; the house necessarily had to provide its own shade since there were not many trees of height at that time. Lowness of pitch encouraged free air circulation, ventilating the interior, and the sharp projections of beams and rafters, which supported the venture, made strong contrasts to the moderate color of the shingles.

The dominant theme of the tract is restraint, with an absence of display and architectural ornament, in fact, with nothing extraneous tacked on but the flower boxes. Yet there exists a sense of the comfort and security one seeks in a home. The street face follows the irregularities of the arroyo edge which were not modified but embraced, even as the stream finds its course along the rocks and rills of the landscape. A particularly handsome stone wall ambles along the face in a sensuous rhythm, evoking the feeling of river flow. Again the brothers appropriate the mossy gray stones from the site for the wall, and warmed and enlivened their gray smooth faces with purplish-brown clinker bricks, those which lie closest to the fire in the kiln and thus bake very hard and burn black in places. Thus the wall is one of unexpected character and softness, although at the time, as Charles remarks, there obviously were some detractors.

A year after the last construction, Charles wrote an article for the *Western Architect* describing what he and his brother had intended and the considerations which had produced the end result.

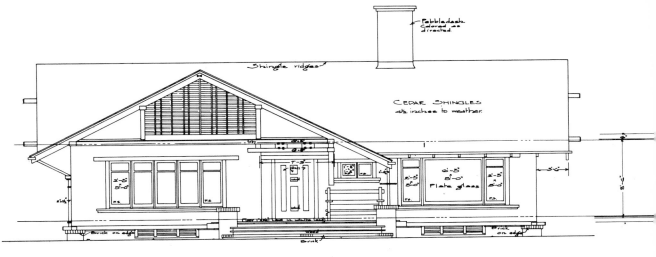

NORTH ELEVATION

The houses here described are in the same neighborhood—in fact are situated side by side on the street called Arroyo Terrace (Spanish arroyo, a small stream). The name is apt. The slope is covered with live oaks down to the valley below, and in the distance in one broad view rise the mountains.

It is unlikely that this land will ever be built upon, probably it will be a park.

This is the outlook that all of these houses have from the front. Most of them are situated above the street. This necessitates terrace walls to give the needed privacy to those who would enjoy the view from out of doors. These walls also protect from the dust of street traffic. The character of these walls was determined upon after a study of the general conditions. A style that admits of freedom from convention will obviously lend itself to this sort of thing. Natural rocks built in with bricks may offend the eye that admits only one cult, or perhaps the eye that is unaccustomed to it may wonder; but time and place should fitly determine a custom of men— the walls I believe serve the purpose for which they were intended.

For the rest, the exteriors of these houses are of common enough materials obtained in local market, but so put together as to warrant their durability and with such ordinary ingenuity and grace as the architects were capable of.

In regard to the practical advantages of casement windows, we have found that a long row of narrow windows gives the best results because one may open any number to gain perfect ventilation without unpleasant draughts. They can be made water tight when hung to swing in or out. We drape them with single heavy curtains that exclude the sun—usually one curtain to each sash but all free to slide upon a pole specially designed so that they may all be drawn to one side if desired.

When these things are designed by the architects it eliminates the cheap flimsy fittings that often mar the best work.

Leaded glass is sometimes used and it is very effective where it seems to fill a real need.

Doors should be interesting in themselves and not merely holes of entrance and exit. This need not make them too conspicuous. For this kind of work batten doors seem very appropriate.

Attention to little things is indispensable to success. I have seen many failures by the want of it.

Hardwood floors seem to fill all of the demands of this kind of house.

Rugs either Oriental or specially designed are most appropriate. Still there are some domestic hand woven fabrics that are good.

The fireplace should be a thing of use. It is

to be deplored that it has at present degenerated into a design for the pressed brick manufacturers. However, steam and furnace may have displaced it. The fireplace from the aesthetic point of view will always be necessary.

A real want always supplies itself with a real thing. Be honest and have no superfluities; is good enough to make a motto.

A real fireplace does heat and does not smoke.

If it does this much it will be appreciated, but to be a real joy it must appeal to our love of the beautiful. The materials have little to do with success. It may be only a sheltered nook with a cosy seat put together with a little thought and love in the effort; perhaps the pleasure of giving others pleasure sawed and hammered and pegged into it all with the passion that makes beauty grow.

[370 Arroyo Terrace—White House] was designed for three unmarried sisters, and embodies their own personal ideas of convenience. The lot was small and of triangular shape with the apex at the back. The house was therefore placed near the street with only a terrace between, and beset in front with a high wall that returned at the west to enclose a wider terrace there. The open rail at top of the wall was designed to allow vines of wisteria to hang over it. It now forms a beautiful sight at the spring of the year. At the

other end the wall steps down to the driveway at the east where a walk from the front door joins it, near the sidewalk. In the rear is a garage, and by its side a little water garden which was designed with studied natural effect. A little pool of lilies and lotus, with grasses overhanging the edges, where gold fish lazily seek the shadows.

On the inside the living room with its book cases and cosy seat by the fireside proved to be homelike and comfortable. In the evening when the fire was lighted this room seemed the proper setting for the little literary evenings that were often held there.

The dining room is wainscotted in deep toned redwood to the height of doors, and hung with a few old prints.

There is a fireplace and on each side of it, a small china closet with doors paneled below and leaded above. The large window in front has a fine view of the mountains. A shelf over the fireplace and china closets hold several Japanese pieces of old Imari blue.

At the east end of the room there is a broad window ledge containing a little aquarium specially designed to accord with the room and its furniture of birch. This latter was treated to harmonize with redwood. The top of the table is finished to use without a cloth, and neither heat nor water will damage it. The rest of the furniture was designed to fit the room.

The bedrooms each have a fireplace. In fact the entire house was heated with open wood fires, and was satisfactory in every way.

The kitchen with its usual accessories was finished in light natural cedar, with walls of cream enamel. The windows hung with white muslin curtains. Altogether it was clean and bright.

Just east of 370, [400 Arroyo Terrace, the Neill house] . . . we will say that it was designed for a certain lady who sold it to a family of three who changed it and added to it to suit its own needs. This kind of alteration always necessitates some incongruities but is interesting. It is of the same materials as Number 1. It may be said that the retaining wall with its field stones is too heavy for the house but it affords the much needed privacy to the little garden overlooking the street.

[408 Arroyo Terrace, the Hawkes House] was designed for a family of eight. This house built of the same material as the preceding, sits lower and consequently has a low wall in front

and is placed further back from the street. The porch which has an open lawn in front of it is well protected by its own wall and affords a delightful place to sit, and as it is on the north side does not cut out the sun. This house has a garage in rear and a raised garden approached by a flight of rough stone steps that lead to a pergola surrounded by cypress trees.

[424 Arroyo Terrace, Willett House] is a small cottage designed for renting purposes. The outside materials are Oregon pine timbers and white cedar shingles without stain. As the house is several years old the whole has weathered into varying tones of warm brown and grey.

The retaining wall in front and the foundation and chimneys are finished in rough pebble dash cement toned slightly darker than the wood but approaching it in color. The private hedge is not yet as high as it was intended.

The front door opens directly into the living room which has a large fireplace of dark brown bricks. The wood work is of Oregon cedar toned brown. The plaster of walls is stained on sand finish a soft brown that is slightly mottled while the ceiling is lighter in same general tone. The electric fixtures were specially designed here as well as in nearly all of the other houses and the same general color tones were used in glass of front door as in the fixtures. Even the curtains and portieres with their fixtures were designed by the architects. It is impossible to describe the harmony that may be obtained when the furniture and fittings are all designed with the house.

[440 Arroyo Terrace, Ranney House] is built of the same materials as Number 4 except the foundations, chimneys, etc. are of dark clinker bricks instead of cement. It rests still lower than the preceding and is placed still further back from the street.

It may be interesting to know that Arroyo Terrace is not a straight street but is an irregular curve from one end to the other, thus no house can be set at a right angle to the street—neither are any of the houses in line, but by careful study this has been compensated for and does not strike the observer as anything unusual.

The fence at the left of [this house] encloses a small clothes yard, etc. There is planting yet to be done to make the front terrace habitable.

[224 No. Grand, Irwin House] is a much larger house than any of the others and was designed for a family of four and guests, etc. The *same general scheme of construction was used and the woods are similar to number 1. The wall in front at the sidewalk is intended to be covered with vines; as it stands, of course, it is out of harmony with the general scheme. This house has a court and fountain in the center and pergola that does not show in the picture. The house is on a corner and is seen from all sides. The trusses that support the porch roof were necessary in order not to obstruct the view from living and dining room windows.*

[368 Arroyo Terrace, Charles Greene's house] is the writer's own house. It was originally built of one story but was added to, to accommodate a growing family. From its high position above the street one has one of the finest views of the Arroyo and mountains. The terrace under the live oak tree is paved with bricks, but among the roots of the tree is a luxuriant growth of ferns. The top of the wall is studded with potted plants and beneath the wide spreading branches is a place arranged for a rustic table and seats.

As Charles has described, within the tract each bungalow was treated as an individual home. Small houses rarely offer much possibility for profound architectural statement, but the architects sought to contain the expressed needs of the client as artfully

as possible. Each was planned to fulfill the economic, domestic and practical considerations of the owner and his piece of land, and the two men executed as many aspects of the design as the client would allow. Given their way, they designed everything, as they were allowed to do in some later commissions. What Charles referred to as "attention to little things" applied to every home they designed, regardless of cost or size. They always concerned themselves with the colors, which they considered a powerful means of expression, using them in exterior finishes to emphasize structure and texture and in the interior to articulate both the interrelations between rooms and between the furnishings and materials that made up each room. Generally, restful earth-toned colors prevailed in various shadings and tones. Rooms were shaded lighter for dark corners, alcoves and the upper part of the room, shaded deeper for sunny areas. Colors also were toned to the position of the house; a northern exposure greeted a warm color scheme and southern light met cooler colors. They designed as many of the fixtures as client and budget would allow: electric fixtures, poles for curtains and drapes, even the curtains and drapes themselves when possible, and they later designed all the furniture as well in their larger and most impressive commissions.

"Fine" and "elegant" as defined by past styles and eras lost their meaning; propriety and simplicity replaced them. Twentieth-century man was no longer under the burden of fitting his American frame into settings and furniture of another period and costume, nor was he now required to enclose himself in a box and order his existence in a closely contained life style in fusty parlors, uncomfortable and unused. Design responded to psychological need, and the accoutrements of another age no longer held sway.

The bungalow which grew from diverse elements, domestic idioms as well as foreign influences, was one of the most significant developments in the American vernacular. For the Greenes it was the testing ground for all that they had taken into themselves to find their own form and identity. It was upon this low art form that they learned to express their artistic sense with a minimum of resources and economy of means. Perhaps this exercise, which required greater effort and imagination, made possible their later work, for to achieve success with few means at one's disposal is the act of imaginative and creative men. In the bungalow the metamorphosis took place and the Greene brothers emerged in 1906, ready for fullest flight into total artistic architectural expression.

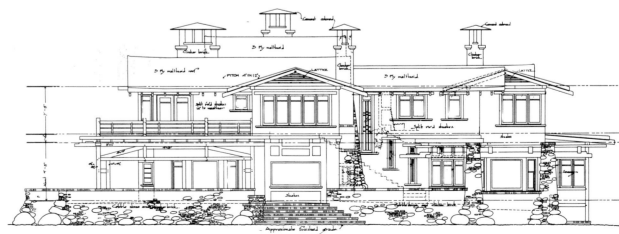

Irwin house, located near Arroyo Terrace, Pasadena;
enlarged in 1906 by the Greenes.
Opposite page: *View of west elevation (photo),
and entrance elevation.*
Left: *Perspective view.*
Below: *View of northwest elevation.*

Right: *Bungalow for Dr. A. A. Libby, Pasadena, 1905. (Demolished.)*

Below: *Elevations and sectional views of residence for Robert Pitcairn, Jr., Pasadena, 1906. (Presently owned by private school.)*

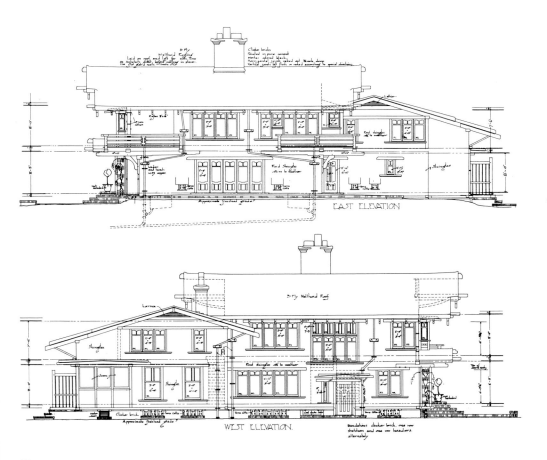

EAST ELEVATION

WEST ELEVATION.

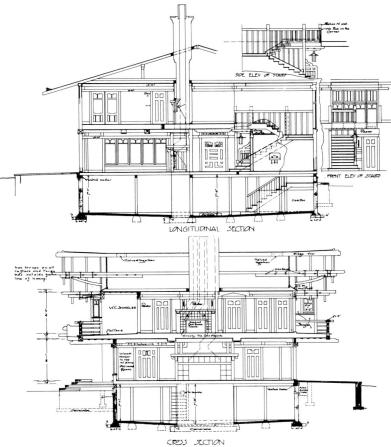

LONGITUDINAL SECTION

CROSS SECTION

Northwest elevation of house done in 1909 for Mr. William W. Spinks. (Restored.)

Retaining wall added to an older house on Arroyo Terrace.
House altered by the Greenes.

Corner window grouping, Louise Bentz House, Pasadena, 1906.
(Sensitively restored to authentic color, woodwork rubbed to original natural finish by present owner.)

23

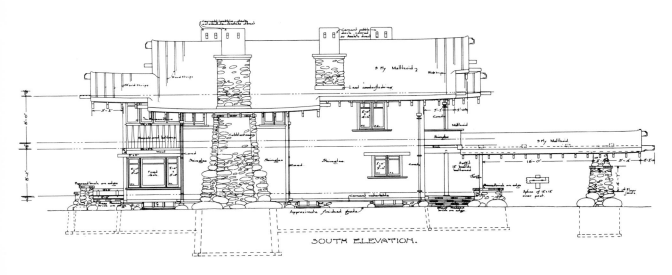

SOUTH ELEVATION.

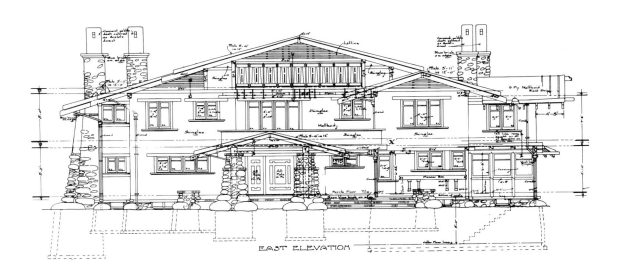

EAST ELEVATION

Mary E. Cole residence, Pasadena, 1907.
(**In altered condition.**)

Cole house; dining room door of quarter-sawed oak with leaded art glass panels.

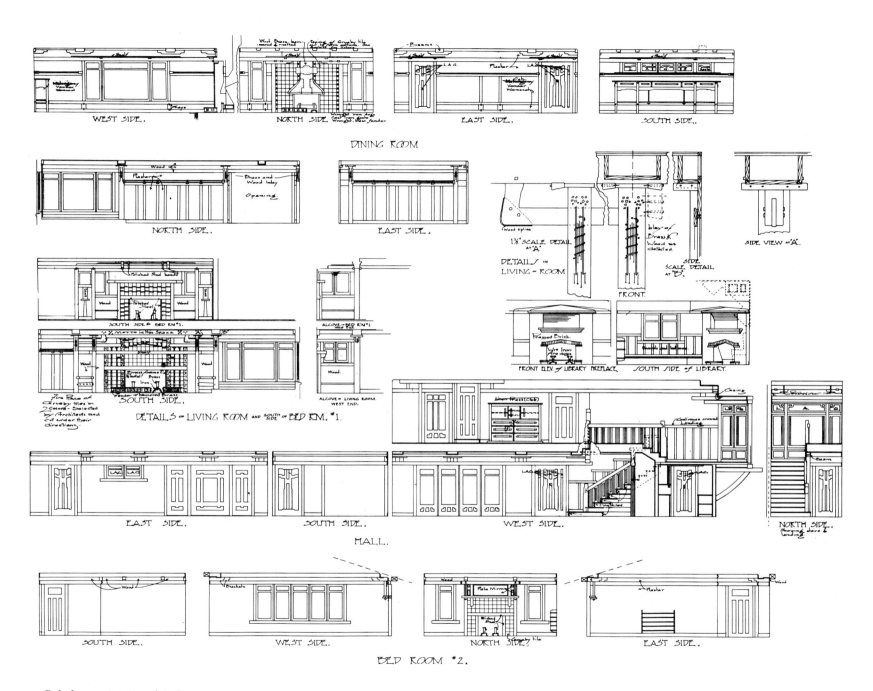

WEST SIDE.   NORTH SIDE.   EAST SIDE.   SOUTH SIDE.

DINING ROOM

NORTH SIDE.   EAST SIDE.

DETAILS in LIVING-ROOM

1½" SCALE DETAIL AT 'A'   SIDE SCALE DETAIL AT 'B'.   SIDE VIEW of 'A'.

FRONT.

SOUTH SIDE of BED RM. #1.   ALCOVE of BED RM #1

SOUTH SIDE.   ALCOVE of LIVING ROOM. WEST END.

DETAILS of LIVING ROOM and SOUTH SIDE of BED RM. #1.

FRONT ELEV. of LIBRARY FIREPLACE.   SOUTH SIDE of LIBRARY.

EAST SIDE.   SOUTH SIDE.   WEST SIDE.   NORTH SIDE.

HALL.

SOUTH SIDE.   WEST SIDE.   NORTH SIDE.   EAST SIDE.

BED ROOM #2.

Cole house; interior details.

25

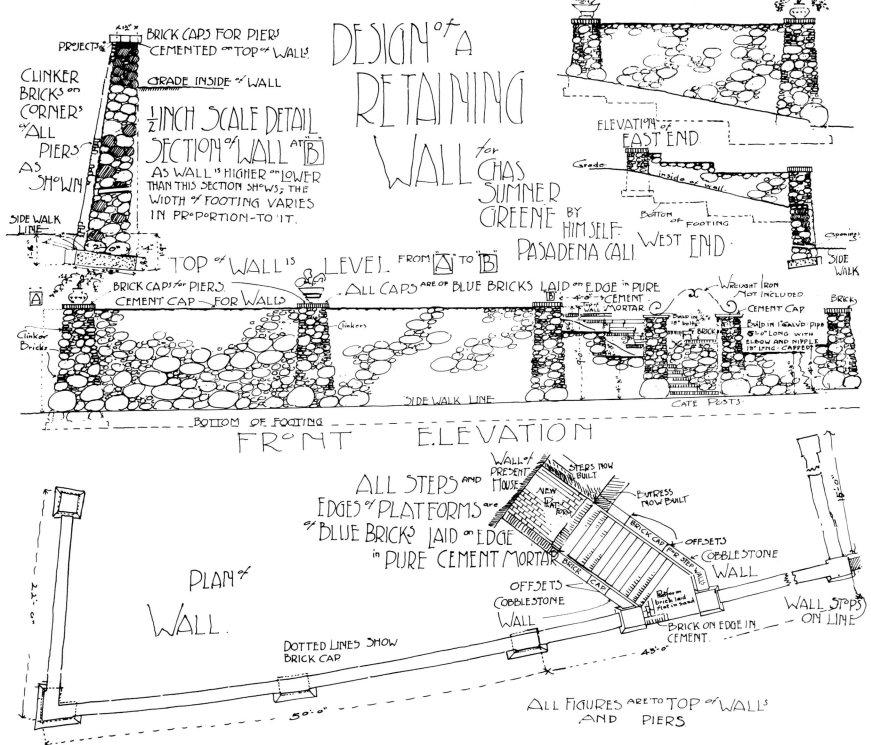

Complete original drawing of retaining wall by Charles Sumner Greene.

Left: *Home of the architect, Charles Sumner Greene,*
368 Arroyo Terrace, Pasadena, begun in 1901.
(Recently restored.)
Above, left: *Master bedroom fireplace.*
Above, right: *Built-in wardrobe in master bedroom.*

Above, left: *Pitcairn house; view from living room.*
Above, right: *Living room, house for William Ladd,
Ojai, 1913 (Restored by owners.)*

Photo, opposite page: *Living room, house for
E. W. Smith, Pasadena, 1910.*

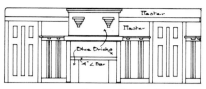

DINING ROOM - NORTH SIDE

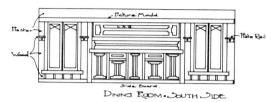

DINING ROOM - SOUTH SIDE

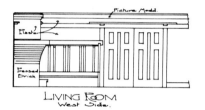

LIVING ROOM
West Side.

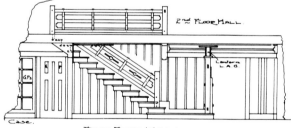

FIRST FLOOR HALL.

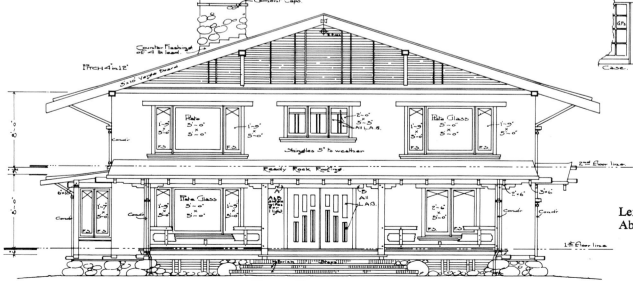

FRONT ELEVATION

Left: *Residence for Mrs. E. A. Ford, Pasadena, 1905.*
Above: *Details of Ford bungalow.*

Right: *Fieldstone chimney of Cole house.*
Opposite page: *Fieldstone chimney of
E. W. Smith bungalow.*

Below, left: *John Blakewell Phillips house, Pasadena, 1906.*
Below, right: *Mary L. Ranney house, 440 Arroyo Ter.*

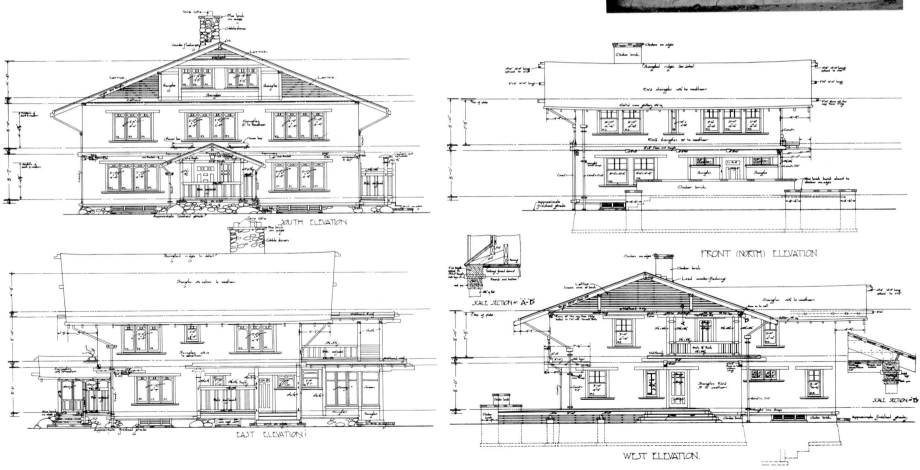

SOUTH ELEVATION

EAST ELEVATION

FRONT (NORTH) ELEVATION

SCALE SECTION AT A-B

SCALE SECTION AT B

WEST ELEVATION.

THE RESIDENTIAL STYLE
Bases of the Residential Style

Commentary on Greene & Greene architecture is based largely upon the commissions commencing from the early 1900s and these homes remain the basis of their reputation. Over the past 60 years they have been variously described and categorized. Some historians have placed their work as the last development in idiomatic American domicile architecture. Another has termed it "neo-stick," its origin lying in the earlier stick style. Others see the brothers' architecture as the supreme expression of the craftsman philosophy, with entire houses of the quality of fine cabinet-making elevated to architectural scale and meaning. Each of these viewpoints is not without some validity, but none expresses or explains the unique character of their creation nor the architectural meaning of their work. It is the intent of this chapter to effect a distillation of the elements that characterize Greene & Greene and thereby extract a more meaningful architectural essence.

True inventions in the architectural usage of wood loom rare in its 5,000-year history of sheltering man and his gods. Only new tools, such as the saw mill, or new methods of connecting timber have changed to any considerable extent the physiognomy of wooden structures. Wood in all its guises from log to planed and polished timber has been a building material throughout the centuries, and the combining and reusing of this common material comprises the history of wood building. American builders and architects figure prominently in this history and have made significant and imaginative contributions in the wooden tradition, which stands as one of America's greatest achievements in architecture, along with inventiveness in steel.

Charles and Henry Greene are very much a part of the American achievement, and perhaps they stand, along with Wright and Maybeck, as the last inventive constructors with the commonplace material, wood. To assess the nature and impact of the brothers' contribution to the wooden vernacular, one must first investigate the milieu in which they created. No understanding of domestic architecture conceived in a certain time and place is possible without also a view of the cultural and social climate in which it took form. Further, the background of the client, the conditions of the contract and the artistic inclinations of the period all have direct bearing upon the final result. So, for the moment, a digression into the bases of the residential style.

Residential communities were the product of the Industrial Revolution; the breakdown of the village, which had been a self-sufficient entity, and the subsequent creation of cities around an industrial hub signaled their appearance. Theretofore, men of wealth created estates and country dwellings; the people lived and work in their community. With the rise of the middle class, however, came the residence —the home laid out on a piece of land by an architect somewhat away from the dust and grime of the city of commerce.

Philosophically, 1900s man was linked to a much earlier age, still living in a solid world under the illusion that moral values, good form and propriety were known and predictable entities. In fact, he was basking in the twilight of a time when knowable values went unquestioned. Intellectually, he knew this, but romantically, he could not accept it. The residence grew out of his romantic notions, not from the idealism he professed nor from his rational existence, which showed business to be a crude, dirty world. By 1900, the populace had a good many politically conservative and socially exclusive men of wealth who took for granted that the destiny of the community, not to mention the country at large, belonged in the hands of the descendants of early Anglo-American Protestant stock, who still believed in solid values. These were the professional men of business who had become wealthy by grace of the vast resources America yielded. It was they who began to map upon the terrain a new style of living that climaxed within a short time in a few prime residential communities.

The residential style was of their making; it sprang from the desire to separate one's private life from the sources which made it possible. The architect-designed house was built for the professional man of business who could afford to commute and thus keep business distinct from what he considered to be his personal values as reflected in his home. He wanted to make his deals as well as to be considered a man of ethics and propriety; the two became harder to reconcile as ugliness and squalor, sweatshops and child labor showed themselves as obvious components of big business.

Thus, the residence became a romantic retreat where women and families were secluded from the ugly aspects of the business world, where a man would return at the end of a day and be assured of his values. In such a setting, his wife could be a woman of leisure and exhibit the cultural values and good breeding that prewar society aspired to; she could do good works without coming into direct contact with those for whom she was doing such acts of charity.

It was a solid world, of knowable proportion and fairly predictable, not the world in flux that we know. Change was taking place at an ever-accelerating rate, but the New England sense of values— thrift and goodness, self-consciousness about wealth and an attendant sense of responsibility for those who were less fortunate—still prevailed. In terms of art, the Puritan attitude still held sway, and the idea of art for art's sake seemed relatively absurd. This attitude tempered greatly the directions in which art was able to express itself in this country. In direct contrast, the Europeans and the British felt fiercely competitive in the field of arts and crafts design on a national level; it was a matter of national pride and interest, and art enjoyed a position in world trade. Americans regarded art as an individual effort, if they regarded it at all, and there was no American design *per se*. It will be remembered that *art nouveau* found expression in America primarily in graphics and in the work of an individual designer, Louis Tiffany, in contrast to the fantastic creations of van de Velde and Makintosh emanating from Europe. The 1900s in Europe saw the work of Baillie, Scott, Voysey, and the Glasgow School of Art, and the modern German and Viennese Secessionists filling the pages of *Studio International,* the British publication, and *Moderne Bauformen,* its German counterpart. Boldly geometric and expressionist in their "decorative construction," the work of Olbrich, Hoffmann, and Bruno Paul was affecting art and architecture on an international scale, breaking with the past and practically usurping Britain's role as the leader of a national arts and crafts movement. They were part of a long tradition in which art and architecture influenced the daily life of people. In America, when Frank Lloyd Wright tried to influence the average citizen's home, he met with apathy. Wright's efforts ultimately depended upon and were supported by clients who were wealthy beyond the norm—and also somewhat non-conformist in view. In fact, Wright's work was recognized and known very early in Europe while remaining relatively obscure on home soil.

The European scene was not without influence on the Greene brothers, despite the time lag of five years that supposedly existed between European taste and that of the East Coast, with five more to pass before new developments reached that poor relative, the West Coast. Charles' trip to England in 1901 placed him in direct contact with the arts and crafts movements and he brought those influences with him to California. It was a turning point in their architectural practice, and the architects Greene set about as builders "employing the process art." In their simplest houses they attempted to make useful objects things of beauty, as William Morris admonished, and therein lies their especial genius. For to make utilitarian objects beautiful without being allowed total freedom and license to do so, and without appreciation or awareness from a client, demands an imagination as great as that

which produced the sensuous undulations of Gaudi and the geometric statements of Makintosh. At every turn, one recognizes the sensuous nature of the artist tempered by Yankee values. The brothers' work from that period could be placed among the finest European and British counterparts of the time, as the British designer, C. R. Ashbee, commented after visiting Charles Greene's studio.

The Greenes' designs took root in the English arts and crafts tradition and carried through to Art Deco. They were creating for a clientele steeped in the Protestant ethic where the sensuous nature of man was suppressed; for people who admired intelligence and good breeding and demanded little or nothing of art except decoration; for a class who aspired to culture and refinement but who were not assured enough in their values to accept anything that seemed extreme. They were philistines, clinging to orthodox tastes for assurance; theretofore, art had been for the aristocracy and was only slowly gaining acceptance. If they knew anything of the events in Europe, they understood little about artistic motivations and movements. Despite this, though they were not themselves artistic, they did have respect for artists as professionals, a respect without which the Greenes and other American artists could not have existed. Not that Pasadena society did not aspire to an interesting life with some flair, but it certainly had to be within the bounds of acceptability and propriety. Within that context, they hired the very best people to create the proper backdrop for their life style, and the architects Greene could meet both the specified and the unrealized needs of these clients. In 1906, they began to receive sizeable commissions to do just that.

From the years 1906 to 1911, a brief moment considering the length of their lives, the brothers burst upon the landscape with a blaze of buildings. It was the flowering of their finest years and these eight or nine homes stand as the great commissions; any one standing alone would be sufficient proof of extraordinary architectural talent. For that brief span of time, they found or were sought by those who could afford to "pay the price of sympathy" for the artist to create, even though clients, by and large, neither fully understood nor realized what they had paid for. Indeed, much of the cost was a price of sympathy for an artist who expended labor on every peg, every fitting, every minute part, which the clients, perhaps, never noticed. Yet there was a limit. The Greenes expended an inordinate amount

of money upon labor rather than the materials themselves, a strange fact when one remembers that the cost of most houses in the 1900s was a 2:1 materials-to-labor ratio, and that the large supply of immigrants made labor relatively inexpensive.

Correspondence with clients and proposed plans and drawings indicate that even with these clients, wealthy beyond the norm, the Greenes were not always allowed to complete their design. In fact, many of the husbands (the house was usually in the wife's name and domain) became more than disgruntled and balked at further expenditures, owing to impatience at the time involved or notions of thrift. Still, it was a moment in time when other restrictions were absent, beyond those imposed tacitly by the nature of the client and his sensitivity toward what they conceived: (1) They were designing for a singular client rather than a mass market. (2) A house was considered neither a speculative venture nor an investment. (3) Clients of those years possessed sufficient means not only to pay cash but to pay for the uncompromising excellence of workmanship which the brothers expended upon their designs. (4) The limit was patience and understanding, seldom cash. Contracts were a matter solely between the client and architect; once the decision was made, there was no subsequent dickering over price. (5) No lending agency or mortgagee stood as intermediary demanding modifications or compromises. Only a building inspector and the client approved the plans, and such considerations as resale value or possible overinvestment did not have to be taken into account. Whereas a financial institution must consider the commercial value of aesthetics, which is usually nil, and the potential market for a house beyond the first owner, the client had only to decide if the architect he hired could interpret the needs and desires of his individual life-style. (6) He accepted, for the most part, the expression of the architect. Given that, in order to make life understandable, human beings necessarily seek the forms that cultural training and background have taught them is home, clients nevertheless were willing to spend an extraordinary amount, above and beyond the norm of the day (it was a pre-income tax era), for the architect to compose a complete home, including the interior furnishings as well as the shell to enclose them. In some cases, the Greenes were even consulted years later by clients who wanted only to change curtains or reupholster furniture. Given certain restraints, architects as yet were unencumbered by outside decorators, a target of continuing complaint by Frank Lloyd Wright, who also believed the architect's domain to be the interior furnishing.

It is of more than passing interest to realize that the Greenes' finest work was commissioned by clients who were variously related. Mrs. Blacker and Mrs. Thorsen were sisters, born of a wealthy Eastern family, and both their husbands were lumbermen. Mrs. Thorsen's Vassar college mate, Mrs. Pratt, was a sophisticated, cultured woman whom a Thorsen relative believes was the mentor in the choice of the Greene brothers, although her own house was the last built of the three. Mrs. Robinson and Mrs. Freeman were sisters and their homes stand side by side, built in 1906 and 1907 respectively. Another Freeman house is found among the Greenes' drawings and plans. A lumberman, James Culbertson, engaged the brothers to do alterations in 1906 on the home they had built for him in 1902 and, in 1911, his three maiden sisters contracted for a large 25-room house. Beyond these relationships, most of the clients were civic-minded men and developed strong mutual affiliations within the community, perhaps an extension of their idealism. For example, the Blackers, Culbertsons and Robinsons contributed large sums to Caltech, and buildings still bear their names.

Thus, clientele, architect and opportunity converged at that moment in time. For the Greenes, there existed for a few short years a nearly perfect climate in which to produce their finest work. Their architectural concepts had ripened and seasoned in earlier buildings and now, both of them still less than 40 years of age, they were about to produce the opus that would mark the acme of their career. It is largely upon the work of those years commencing in the early 1900s that their reputation is based and upon which most historians draw for evaluation.

Although lives and careers rarely demarcate themselves into neat calendrical divisions, some significant and marked characteristics became apparent in their work from 1906. Their work began to assume a larger dimension and achieved fuller expression. For that brief moment in time, all the conditions seemed optimum. Now they were allowed to exhibit an originality of design in each house that extended to the furnishings without having to consider the cost of producing one of a kind. They could choose a unique design motif around which the house and materials revolved, and order custom-made items to carry out the theme. In interior design, their work was comparable to that of Charles Mewes and Arthur Davis, famous in Europe at that time as interior architects of hotels and ocean liners; like them, they carried out their artistic concepts to the smallest detail. Greene & Greene had become a large enough firm to supply a local mill and contracting firm with sufficient business to work for the brothers exclusively; thus they could order materials to their specifications rather than fit their plans to standardized measurements.

With a command of both craft and building principles, there evolved in their work a structural expressionism that heightened the sense of form and design—where a detail becomes part of the orchestration of the whole. Their architecture began to communicate a different spatiality, though within the confines of man's philosophically solid world of the 1900s. "Three," wrote Charles, "is pre-eminently the number of architecture, because it is the number of our space, which is three-dimensional, and architecture is most concerned with spatial relations. The division of a composition into three related parts is so universal that it would seem to be the result of an instructive *actiori* of the human mind."

Two disparate sources which shared the common structural quality of a visual appearance of structure, became apparent as the Greenes evolved toward their own structural expressionism. They were the English half-timber frame and the Japanese cage. For most architectural firms, the country home in the English manner had been a stock-in-trade item for years. It was a popular style, evidenced by frequent illustrations of the cottage or country house in magazines ranging from the *Ladies Home Journal* to *Studio International*. It appealed not only to those who affected the cultural values of the British and wanted an image of respectability and propriety, but psychologically the country home reflected the American's ideal of home—a haven of unquestioned values and quietude, harking back to another age; a reminiscence of village life in a country setting. Half-timber houses, based on medieval Britain's timber-framed structures, had a different architectural message for the Greenes, which Charles had received first-hand on his trip to England. The firm built a full timber-framed house for Mrs. Adelaide Tichenor in 1906, translating the influence into terms of structural vitality as opposed to picturesque effect. To express the sense of structure that the original timber frames imparted, the house required an elaborate network of false construction which mere picturesqueness did not demand. They wove diagonal braces into the fabric of the exterior; they constructed post and beam in convincing support; they applied pegging and bracketing to affirm structural truth. But only the form could be approximated; in substance it was not the same. The vitality and truth of the medieval timber frame sprang from structural members—cruxes in the shape of natural tree bends and irregular beams that strayed from the plumb—jointed and pegged with wooden nails. The frame retained a feeling of the forest and still seemed to be within organic life even though forced into man-made geometries. Visually the structural sense derived from its irregularity and kinship to the tree. One intuitively trusted that the house was strong, even though a beam might sag or a post lean. Once rough-hewn, irregular forms assumed the evenness and abstraction of lumber, the tree—the life process —died.

Yankee craft sought to eradicate tree origins and to make timber shipshape. A sense of fitness and the thin, crisp line was a craftsman's pride, exemplified by the ship craft of Mainers. The Yankee builder valued neatness and economy rather than artistry, and his sense of the land and nature was not akin to that of medieval man, who felt his life intertwined with the forest for existence. Thus, neither form nor technique was truly adaptable to American methods, particularly in the structural sense in which the Greenes sought expression. They designed two very large, impressive structures in the half-timber vein and altered a third which they had built in 1902, houses which are beautifully executed, visually pleasing structures. They are as successful an adaptation of the style as one can find, but the brothers were still seeking their expression and their sights turned to the Orient.

The brothers were following a well-traveled path. Fenollosa, Hearne and Morse, all of Bostonian heritage, had looked to the Orient. They had sought to combine the sense of mystery and sensuality of the oriental culture with their Bostonian upbringing and American sense of practicality, evolving free and inventive life styles. The Greenes had long been acquainted with the East and had used, as had most architects at some time in their careers, decorative elements of the Orient in their work. Their superficial interest in the decorative, however, evolved into a profound involvement with the structural bases of Japanese architecture. These principles infused their own architectonic expression and stimulated their inventive spirits to their finest and most original designs.

Essentially Japanese buildings were a cage, the structural essence of the American balloon frame. Japanese architects believed that structure, that is, cage structure, derived from both architectural and natural sources; for them, seeing the essence of structure led one to perceive the structure of reality. Form was neither arbitrary nor imposed by circumstance of material and place; cage structure was the inevitable form which had evolved, in the Japanese mind, not only from geometric and physical principles, but aesthetic ones as well. It resolved multiple forces into a basic rectangular form that both inner contemplation of nature and centuries of skill revealed to them, and they preserved the cage, sometimes using only paper for walls.

The balloon frame was also a cage, but it had never been used as such. In the long-established Western tradition of conceiving a building as walls or facades, the inherent qualities of the balloon frame were ignored; it was used simply as a shell upon which to drape one style or another. A majority of all houses built up to the 1900s were constructed by this method, which consisted of nailing 2x4-inch sticks, placed at 16-inch intervals, to a supporting beam, another 2x4 stick. By driving nails in askew, the frame had incredible durability and strength and it was capable of being forced to any sham style, often seeming more stage set than home. Visually, the balloon-framed home appeared unsubstantial and unconvincing as support. The thin flesh of wall sidings applied to a raw-boned skeleton disquieted the senses, hence the epithet "ticky tack" applied to the American house. "Even today," wrote the critic Sigfried Gidieon in the 1950s, "the European observer finds their thinness really daring;" the European eye was trained on a tradition of massive stone walls. It was true; even intellectual understanding of the solid engineering basis of support and strength did not satisfy the visual need for the appearance of stability and permanence. Only during constructional stages did the balloon frame appear the structural entity it in fact was, only then was it visually exciting, like the raw-boned steel cages of modern buildings. It lost its validity as soon as the structure was hidden and the spatiality disappeared.

The Greenes constructed most of their houses using this rudimentary construction technique, but they began to use the balloon frame as cage, preserving it beneath a sheathing of shingles and

emphasizing the essential geometric order. They exploited the inherent qualities which the Europeans found disturbing—the elegant thinness and rib-like skeletal appearance—extending the members beyond the walls to further imply the geometry. They underscored the stick appearance of the Western frame house and placed the sticks in rhythmic, linear progressions to create real space and establish subtle, changing relationships. Most vitally, inherent in the concept of preserving the cage, they relieved the skeleton frame of the visual necessity to hold up the building, though not of the actual need, and thereby freed the frame from its visual burden of support. Now the cage could be a cage. They accomplished this by transferring supremacy to the roof—the dominating form in a Greene & Greene house, visually independent, almost indifferent to the walls that actually support it.

Such massive roofs involved a great amount of engineering; they were not simply a natural outcropping of form. Though retaining suggestions of Japanese and Swiss prototypes, the Greenes lowered the profile, in some houses to near horizontality, spreading the roof wider and extending it farther. It is the essential element of shelter in any house and in Greene & Greene, it is the key to the spatial concept as well. It is a space structure. Unlike Mies van der Rohe, and Le Corbusier, for whom the roof became merely a deck with the walls assuming the responsibility for spatiality, or Neutra, who created his spaces with interpenetrating walls and free-standing planes with no bays, the Greenes established space with a massive roof that throws its influence far beyond the walls and visually frees the movement beneath. From the inside of the house looking outward one is aware of the interpenetration of the roof through the wall, the beams reaching from inside out. The roof seems ready to rise, possessing a lift, the splines of rafters like the wing of a bird. Perhaps it was the artist perceiving the new era of flight, forms which had been given birth only a few years before at Kitty Hawk; standing in the attic of the Gamble House, one can almost feel oneself airborne.

Greene & Greene roofs also assumed various configurations, sometimes used in combination or as multi-faceted, interrelated planes. They were modeled, proportioned and textured with sculptural sensitivity and architectural spatiality so that, in each of the major houses, the roof is the decisive element to which all other elements are orchestrated. A variety of materials, from tiles to common asphalt

roofing paper, composed the cap, with wooden splines extending from the inside of the house beyond the roof in support. They became light-breakers, filtering the sunlight through their fingers and creating shadow-play across the shakes, making light an element of decoration. No sharp edges exist, for sharp edges give a feeling of hollowness; every beam end is rounded and thus every structural member seems supportive and heavier. Surface becomes one and continuously turns upon itself and changes direction without pause. Rounded, sculpted beam ends emphasize grain and the fibrous quality of wood as well, supporting the sense of solidity; end grain is exposed, capturing and softening the sun's rays as well as lending its own sense of sculptural support.

Within the context of building to satisfy visual and psychological requirements—to impart a sense of structure—the Greenes added an incredible multiplicity of structural elements, the ultimate charm of which is that one is not aware of the principles involved.

To express a sense of structure, the Greenes employed elementary techniques of the builder's art reminiscent of man's primeval will to form—the post and beam, the truss, the corbel, the bracket. They skillfully wove them into the psychological fabric of structure, although they were superfluous from a structural standpoint. Post and lintel—most basic to man since he first piled one stone upon another—evolved into an architectonic element of mutitudinous form. The Greenes transformed the post into batten and column, reinforcing and reiterating structure. The truss, a diagonal piece between two structural members and usually used in roof support, appears throughout interior and exterior. Brackets appear consistently, used to hold up imagined and real structure, bolstering a beam or standing as rafter foothold. Corbelling became another important element which the Greenes inventively wove into their visual structure. As used by the Swiss, corbelling imparted both structural vitality and decorative possibilities and the Greenes adapted the technique to interior expression as well. Beam overlays beam, each extending beyond the last. It becomes an oft-used transitional element from column to beam, both strengthening and softening the meeting of post and lintel; it supports the horizontals, intensifying continuous space. In their most abstract application, corbelled beams compose the stairway of the Gamble House.

Once the structural form evolved, it became the

marrow from which architectural design and expression took life. It became bare bones and luxurious flesh in one, ornament rather than extraneous application, the articulation of structure itself. The main architectural developments in Japan, once the inevitable form was resolved, had been in the articulation of structure, and the Greenes, too, began to articulate structure as an expression of art. Charles defined it as "structural necessity made beautiful . . . architecture is the necessarily useful made pleasurable." To articulate as well as to build structure, the Greenes used the same vocabulary as the carpenter and cabinet-maker. But their approach to craft was that of the aesthete as well as that of the craftsman. They perceived the design elements behind the technique and focused upon the abstractions inherent in even simple joinery. Craft was the tool for the expression of the idea rather than the idea itself.

Joinery was a trademark of the American home and the Greenes used a variety of common methods to join two pieces of wood together. The scarf joint became their trademark. In every room of each of the large houses and in most of their smaller houses, a scarf joint is articulated. Theretofore it had been a carpenter's, as opposed to cabinetmaker's, common and widely-used technique for joining structural members both in exterior and interior construction; it was rarely exposed. There were several variations of the scarf, the Japanese using it on a diagonal, but the Greenes based their design on a parallelogram which moved from right at the top, to left at the base, with a center line following the board line. Two pieces of wood with shaped, overlapping ends join to form one continuous piece without increased thickness; the joint is locked by wedges or keys to resist tension. The Greenes adapted the design of the two-wedge lock so that one end presented a continuous, rounded face of either oak or ebony, and the scarf became a kinetic element, breaking the monotony yet maintaining continuity. The peg declared a third dimension to the flat board surface.

A multiplicity of mortise and tenon joints were also extensively used. A mortise is a space hollowed out in a timber to receive a projection, the tenon. Usually of rectangular cross section, the tenon at the end of a piece of timber fits into the mortise socket to make the joint. "Stub tenons," which project only part way into the timber, are hidden joints, pinned originally with wooden pegs or wedges. The Greenes used screws, boring into the end piece to create patterns of design, and then

covering the screw heads with ebony inserts. "Through-tenons" pierce the mortised timber and show on the other side; they appeal visually, but weaken a member more than the stub. The Greenes used them less than they imitated them, often attaching a piece for the appearance of a through-tenon, adding a sense of three dimensions.

One of their unique adaptations of a joinery technique was of the box-joint, generally used for precisely that—to make a box. They, however, used it on an architectural scale, leaving the edges to overlap, rather than cutting them flush where the members meet. Used in this way and on this scale, the box joint becomes a three-dimensional joint eliminating the abrupt and sharp corner. With the end grain exposed and the ending of one member enfolding the other, the meeting becomes a rounded form and the opposing angle is softened.

Dovetail joints, a tapered form of the mortise and tenon, belong in the province of the cabinet and furniture maker as well, and the Greenes used these joints less for visual purpose than they did for structural necessity, particularly in their furniture. So-named because the tenon expands in width toward the tip and resembles the fan-like form of the tail of a dove, this joint is the most exacting to make and is the trademark of a fine joiner. A variation of the dovetail, the double-socket feather joint, found its way into some of the houses in a resemblance to a butterfly, the tenon often of a darker-toned wood and quite lyrical in prospect.

Tongue-and-groove, the joint generally used for flooring was also standard with the brothers. In this joint the tongue is formed on the edge of one of the pieces to be joined, the groove in the other.

Another favored structural element was metal straps. Necessary for strength, metal bandings secured wooden members together. Their cold metal strength created striking contrasts to the soft warm wood, again expressing inherent material values. Pegs, both round and square, were used extensively in a variety of ways. Practically, some covered heads of screws which held structural members firm, and everywhere tiny square pegs obtruded ever so slightly, in linear progression along a beam or grouped in patterns of design. On a larger scale, false pegs were often intruded where two planar boards met. Emulating the scarf joint wedge, these rectangular pegs were slightly rounded on the edges and softened the abrupt severity of the meeting of two unrelieved straight lines. Set into the line of meeting by chamfered incisions, the pegs also suggested

dimensionality; thus the planar surface took on a sense of depth, which Frank Lloyd Wright considered a fourth dimension in the interplay of volumes: "It is this quality of depth that alone can give life to architecture; one must be able to sense and feel thickness." The brothers used pegs of ebony as well, the black color creating accents to the warm tones of the wood. On occasion, small pegs of oak were used, nearly flush with the surface, confirming or establishing direction.

In a Greene & Greene house every visible structural member is articulated; some become art forms, so sensitively molded and sculptural are they. Were there nothing but the Gamble House stairway or the landing post of the Blacker stairwell remaining, it would suffice as evidence of an artist. In the most unexpected places a sculpted form appears, such as the kingpin in the Gamble House attic. The articulation of architectonic elements found boundless outlets. There is a fantastic complication and multiplication of parts, each articulated, each with an individual identity, that could lend interminable descriptive material. The Greenes expended attention to every item as perhaps no other American architects have ever done, and one is surprised at every turn at one more detail, previously missed. Such lavish attention given to the smallest detail has been little understood. Some historians have explained it as love of craft; others have believed it the work of a fanatic perfectionist; less-enamored observers have seen it as a ridiculous exercise in minutiae. The enormous expenditure of labor on an incredible number of details can only be understood in terms of architectural meaning, for the tedious work necessary to execute each detail would hardly have appealed to the brothers were it just for the sake of craft.

What the Greenes worked to express through a multiplicity of parts was a total concept of architectonic expression. They constructed a home much as a painter might construct a painting, building a composition and working first to produce harmonies of line, mass, space and color, then to build simple harmonies into higher forms. Within that framework, the detail became a note in the creation of a harmony; harmonies existed to dramatize and express a total concept, much as tonal gradations, compositional geometries and brush-stroke velocities contribute larger meanings to a painting of a simple theme. Charles called it the "Law of Consonance: Thus it may be seen that in a work of art as in a piece of tapestry, the same thread runs through the web, but goes to make up different figures. The idea is deeply theosophic: one life, many manifestations; hence, inevitably, echoes, resemblances—Consonance."

In the detail is the germ of the whole. Elements do not blend into an indistinct collective; each functions as a complete entity and is as perfect within itself as it could be made. It maintains an appointed function for itself, one of the many manifestations of the architectural expression.

Throughout their work, the Greenes displayed a mastery of what might be termed the third element. One becomes increasingly aware of another element or force that brings two materials together, that softens the opposition when two straight lines meet, that adds a third dimension when two planes come together.

They are masters of modulation, changing rhythms or directions, tones and gradations, proportions or angles with infinite subtleties of design. They affect harmonious phrasings among elements and groupings with a virtuosity that makes it almost unnoticeable, sometimes using the simplest elements to accomplish difficult transitions. A rounded edge softens the severity of abrupt right angles and buffers the junction of straight lines. Sawmill angularity dissolves into the fine curve, effecting the change from one condition to another. Batten meets board with cushioned edges, however slight the rounding may be; post joins beam with rounded connections. The curve speaks to the sensuous nature of man, tempering his puritanical carpentry. Changes of plane and direction become plastic transitions and Yankee linear uprightness is mellowed and blended by the slightest suggestion of a curve. The dual nature of elements and dissimilar materials is recognized and brought into equilibrium, even as Charles in later life sought to resolve man's duality into oneness with the universe.

At every turn, one senses a subtle change from dark to light, from lower to higher, from rigidity to elasticity and stillness to movement. Such power to play upon one's associations creates a bridge between abstract architectural values and human sensory experience. One intuitively feels a balance between the elements, with connections becoming harmonic phrasings, establishing an affinity among elements of similar or dissimilar nature. Transitions quietly assert change—of direction, form, scale—without jarring the composition; the detail joins basic elements into larger entities of different proportion and meaning. Their vocabulary is rich and varied to

effect the change—of joints, connections, details. It would seem remarkable enough were all these details designed and spelled out in copious plans but they were not. The Greenes constructed within a broad system of organizational principles and constants that allowed them maximum flexibility and exercise of ingenuity. Such freedom was supported by men of crafted skill who could exert their talents with minimal instruction. It is interesting to note the reaction to the Greenes' structural approach by a distinguished architect of the time, Ralph Adams Cram:

One must see the real and revolutionary thing in its native haunts of Berkeley and Pasadena to appreciate it in all its varied charm and its striking beauty. Where it comes from heaven alone knows, but we are glad it arrived, for it gives a new zest to life, a new object for admiration. There are things in it Japanese; things that are Scandinavian; things that hint at Sikkim, Bhutan, and the fastness of Tibet, and yet it all hangs together, it is beautiful, it is contemporary, and for some reason or other it seems to fit California. Structurally it is a blessing; only too often the exigences of our assumed precedents lead us into the wide and easy road of structural duplicity, but in this sort of thing there is only an honesty . . .
but an honesty, "that is sometimes almost brazen."

Frank Lloyd Wright might be said to have approached architecture from the cavity, with the enclosing of spaces as the basis of architectural form and the order one of imposed geometry. The Greenes' approach to architecture was through materials—the giving of form to materials, so that they became the vehicle of expression, with the ultimate form deriving from the articulation thereof.

Wood was the essential material of both interior and exterior construction of their first houses and commentary over the years on Greene & Greene houses revolves around their use of wood. Implied or stated in every appraisal of their work has been the assumption that they loved wood, that first material delivered by the forces of Nature. But if they approached building through materials, through wood, the idea, nevertheless, was first. "All science points to the conclusion that nothing endures but ideas—material either expresses ideas or ideas cause material. We may never know which, but that does not matter now to us. We do know that life molds materials and creates something that did not exist (by means of ideas), therefore intelligence puts ideas first." Their ideas took wooden forms because

wood was incredibly abundant as were the men who knew how to work with it.

When the Pilgrims stepped upon the shores of the New World they could not have known that it supported 937 million acres of virgin forest of great variety. What they did know was that as far as the eye could see, trees prevailed, and in their minds as in the minds of most Americans, there was the certainty of a supply to last "forever." Out of that frail imagining, glimpsed as seemingly endless tree tops, came the vernacular building material from which American architecture established its birthright and in which tradition the Greenes continued. Because of its abundance, it was bent to every real and imagined use. Rare was the man in America's early days who did not have some experience with carpentry or carving. As the Sears, Roebuck catalog plainly reveals, in 1908, wood was incredibly cheap and could be exploited for innumerable purposes. Such diverse items as washing machines for $6.38, view cameras with holders for upwards of $13.00, washboards with tenon joints, and even beehives with dovetailed joints for $7.68 were made of wood. Furnishings—chairs as cheap as 69¢, bedsteads for as little as $2.35 and refrigerators from $4.45 up—were available to everyone, and more or less expensive depending upon the amount of ornamental design and carving included. Wood was the obvious building material to use.

Although cement was more truly an indigenous material, for Pasadena and most of Southern California abounded in sand and gravel, the technology to make cement was in its infantile stages and even then, the psyche was not attuned to its use. Secondly, an abundant supply of craftsmen who knew how to work with wood were available and could be relied on to carry out with craft what the brothers were seeking to express architecturally. The Greenes found their craftsmen counterparts in two brothers named Hall, and apparently the relationship among the four was one of mutual resepct and equanimity, an ideal one between artist and builder. The Halls made the Greene's designs possible; the Greenes' requirements made possible the master craftsmanship of such skilled men as the Halls.

Peter and John Hall were born the sons of a cabinetmaker in Sweden. The family's first American dwelling was in Illinois where the father taught his craft to his sons in the old country tradition. When they knew their trade and had gathered sufficient capital, they started their own contracting company and mill with John managing the mill and Peter in charge of running the business. During the Greenes' prime years, the Halls handled the brothers' contracts exclusively, for they rivaled the Greenes in their standards of excellence and quality. Their business was founded on the highest quality craftsmanship just as the Greenes' architectural practice was based upon absolute integrity. Moreover, the Halls had a retinue working for them who were also European-trained in the true tradition of craftsmanship, and who could work not only in wood but stone and metal as well. Workmen are not designers, but they could understand Charles' instructions and carry them out with precision. Because of the brothers' background in the craft, they understood what could be done with wood and how to utilize the talent of these men to the fullest extent.

The manner in which the Greenes used wood and unique expressions they created with that common material sprang from a higher idea, from the heart of art itself. Charles considered, in regard to all materials, not only wood, that the "qualities that make a material useful rarely make it interesting. The quickened sensibility and imagination of the artist must do that. Sensibility infers a reaction to every quality of the substance—imagination to the utilization of its qualities to create the emotion in the beholders that the artist felt. Elusive and vague, or clear and strong—all things for all minds." Architecturally, their approach placed them among the "progressives," wrote Alan McGowan, those "who wanted to bring out the 'real' character of these materials, to design shapes and plans 'natural' to them, whether it was the structural character of the steel cage as in Sullivan's tall buildings, the smooth whiteness and sculptural possibilities of poured concrete in Gill's houses, the roughness of stucco as Maybeck used it, or the infinite variety of oiled, roughed, jointed effects achieved by the Greenes in redwood."

With the artistic sensibilities of the Greenes, wood became a tree reborn, yielding its inner abstract aspect without relinquishing its nature and character as a living substance. Every quality of the once-tree was utilized. Grain became the stuff of aesthetic visions. A tree takes its sustenance and growth and recreates it in the form of rings or layers, even as we create the lines and wrinkles on our faces, and thus grain is a retelling of the life process. As the struggle for survival in hard, cold winters or drought of summers leaves its mark in the bands, grain becomes more expressive. As the brothers used it, grain revealed tree life,

suggesting the kinetic force within as it changed patterns and direction with the changing light of day. Crossing grains on horizontal and vertical members suggest the dual aspect of wood, seeming to change from firmness to softness as the daylight shifts. End grain, so abused or hidden by carpenters, ran into length grain, turning upon itself and creating continuity of surface.

Structurally, wood assumes a solid rather than surface appearance, just as the tree. Paneling, both supportive and nonsupportive, never looks applied: again, articulation versus application.

Various species of wood were used in every house by the Greenes. No two kinds of wood are identical, and no two pieces of the same species of wood are exactly the same. A tree grows like a human being, possessing the inheritance of its parents' seed, yet building singularly its own cells and structure, once planted. With that individuality, the Greenes created mysterious and beautiful relationships, "all things for all minds."

In the use of natural finishes, color, and textures of wood, derived from nature herself, Greene and Greene houses re-established the connection with nature. Any further gesture to blend architecture with nature was redundant and a self-conscious attempt at rusticity. Exterior walls were sheathed with 36″ wooden shakes, with 12″ exposed to the weather. Dipped in creosote stains for varying periods, depending upon the color effect sought, they took on gray-green hues of various shadings, becoming as native to the landscape as the greens and browns of earth and oak. In time the shakes obtained a textural richness and depth, each a distinct piece of broken color in an almost pointillistic effect, blending into an impressionistic wall. Depending upon opposition and contrast, the wall changes its facade with the shifting sunlight. Shingles were cut with an uneven end called a log butt, rather than square, so that the ends became slightly bent and twisted with weather and became craggy light traps. The inherent texture, maintained and enhanced by the stain, provides one of the basic clues to scale and dissolves the monolithic facade of the wall to human proportion, adding visual interest at close range. Roughness of form emphasizes structure where smooth surfaces conceal it.

Exterior wooden members—rafters, purlins, posts and beams—assume the roundness and grain that the tree imparts, becoming more akin to natural forms. Here the sawmill quality of a board which denounces tree origins is also absent.

Imagination molded every material into shapes and patterns natural to it, on its own scale and in its own condition. The artistry lies in the contrasts and relationships created between the inherent qualities and in the harmonies brought about between natural colors and textures. Each material maintains its identity, stated clearly, yet with a sense of value beyond itself, becoming more than itself. There is a sense of the spiritual emanating from the material; the universal in the particular, just as the Japanese choose one rock to signify the mountain. It has its distinct, individual nature "rock," yet it transcends its meaning without the design and function inherent to its nature being violated. Thus, the integrity of materials contributes part of the larger meaning to a Greene & Greene structure, the meaning of art where things are more than themselves.

In plan, most Greene & Greene houses appear to be straightforward and simple. They derive from the early eighties, and they relate to the open, flexible, sprawling plan of shingle-style houses which Richardson so masterfully designed. They are not, however, loose, unemphatic compositions as they have sometimes been described. The organizational principle upon which the plan revolves is that of asymmetry and the plan of a Greene & Greene house reveals itself as one begins to move around it. It was conceived with each line, volume and space influenced by and creating spatial relationships with every other. The graceful interplay of proportions and rhythm of forms is less visible at the outset than the immediate outline. Understood as a fluid process where form is extendable *ad infinitum,* the plan becomes exciting; it is only fully realized when one participates in the completion.

When ordering is asymmetrical, its vitality depends upon the active mind to realize momentary wholeness, only to dissolve it again into another form. Visually, the plan dies if considered complete. Asymmetry to the Japanese meant incompleteness so that it was within the process of life (the Way). Considered a finality or would-be symmetry gone astray, the plan indeed becomes unauthoritative and suggests disequilibrium. When one contributes to it one's experience, its essence is life, growth, change and relatedness, implying relationships beyond itself.

In their plans, open space is as important as the enclosed space, much as it is in Islamic architecture, and the house often has as much as one-third additional space in usable half-open, half-enclosed porches, for both day and night use. Porches become an integral part of the total volume, and the interaction of the void with the elements that define it is never static. Space surrounding the house is treated as part of the plan and is modulated. From the craggy monolith of the wall one is led to the geometric progression of post and beam and then to the garden and the infinite beyond; from the clarity of geometric structure imposed by exposed structural beams, to the vague, undefined forms of nature. Amidst the primeval form of post and lintel and the essential geometric order, one is surrounded by undulating lines, and patios and verandas which reach out multi-directionally from the house like a plant spreading its tendrils; from perfection of form to sheer invention.

The brothers designed from precision to dissolution, outlining by implication and suggestion man's will to form. They created rhythmic progressions in the multiplication and placement of beams, where shape-shifting spaces come into being as one moves about the house. The essence of the plan is flux, a fluid movement along, through and around the plan. Insofar as they were able to place the house on a sizable plot of land, their houses come alive in a myriad of vistas. They composed their masses in nature's perspective as a painter builds a picture, but they could do it in all directions, so that a view or vista from every part of the house, if possible, was planned.

The approach is unimposing and rarely direct, providing a sense of arrival in an intimate and casual way, rather than a grandiose entry. Such indirect entrances, sometimes by way of curving driveways or through an interior court, mediate between the noise and crush of external avenues and the privacy and quiet of being in a friend's domain.

Every house is a series of elevations between the powerful horizontals, earth and roof, with the sky providing the dynamic element of ever-changing light. In some cases, incredible changes in elevation from front to rear exist, stabilized by the wide-spreading, all-embracing roofs of Greene & Greene invention. Their elevations become conformations to the land, which the Greenes shaped into knolls and slopes to achieve varying viewpoints of nature. Every house rested within such a controlled setting. There is no attempt to make a house one with nature, as Frank Lloyd Wright often was wont to do, most notably in Falling Water. Their homes exhibit no such enthusiastic interpenetration of man's forms with nature's. Though cited as forerunners of indoor-outdoor living and the California life style, in fact, their concept was quite opposite, for

they sought to mediate man's position in nature, realizing the interdependence of man and nature yet acknowledging the fact that man does not directly relate to nature—he is no longer a creature of tree and forest. Always there exists a contrast between the forms of nature and those wrought by the mind and hand of man. By creating orderly progressions from interior to exterior, from the fabricated to arranged natural elements, even as the Japanese did in their rock and sand gardens, they tried to come to terms with the differences, to make it possible for man to perceive nature and ultimately, perhaps, to understand it. Toward that end, they made many gestures.

Gardens were an important feature of every Greene & Greene house. They stood as persuaders of nature, as the mediating element between the geometric architectural rhythms of the house and the infinite rhythms of rock, tree and mountain. Gardens assumed nature's ordered and pleasurable aspects, contrived for man's appreciation, and they are an inherent part of the definition of the residential style. Through them, man had the possibility of establishing a link with the natural world.

Almost every Greene & Greene house has an arbor, providing a place of shade and rest, sheltering one from the blaze of the same sun that fired the bloom of the bright flowers. "A secluded spot," described Charles Greene, "sheltered but not gloomy where one may leave one's book or work and take it up again at will." Pergolas, too, are found in almost all of the major plans, some of them quite elaborate and carved. Pergolas stretched cool arms over white-skinned faces, for suntanning the skin was unthinkable.

Patios and terraces laid in 8-inch square mission tiles composed large flat planes spreading from the house. From the square abstraction of these areas, the Greenes led to the garden by a change of direction and scale. They dissolved the geometry of square and diamond into intricate flat brick of undulating patterns and then into the rock itself. The rock with its unchangeable solidity, from whence all life took hold, becomes a link between plant life and buildings, the transition from abstract to organic, from man-made abstractions and textures to the natural. Stairs from the patio are angled to the garden and to each other, avoiding the severity implicit in the meeting of straight lines. One is persuaded to change direction and viewpoint rather than face the garden squarely; the change is subtle, an implied rhythm directed by

the curved placement of stairway and a sense of surprise at what awaits around the corner. At every turn one is provided with a focal point, so that a space is not formless and undifferentiated. One is given a point of reference, a humanly-scaled object or element, by which to relate himself to the infinite. Lanterns, urns, and pots, all designed by the Greenes, bring the larger order into scale and establish wider relationships in space; plants and trees also accomplish the humanism of nature by strategic placement. Always there is a suggestion, an implication of the infinitude of nature and a greater force brought to human understanding. The life-giving elixir of water is contained in lily ponds, bird baths and fountains. And in everything there is a sense of proportion that is almost a divine gift, which brings about subtle transitions from the man-made to the natural, that makes changes a continuous ebb and flow rather than stops and starts.

Interiors evoke a rhythmic melodic sense of continuity throughout. Amidst quiet yet constant surprises of subtly changing directions and advancing and receding planes, there is a continuity given by the stability of the horizontal line. C. R. Ashbee, a leading figure in the English arts and crafts movement and contemporary with the Greenes, described their interiors thus:

I think C. Sumner Greene's work beautiful; among the best there is in this country. Like Lloyd Wright the spell of Japan is on him, he feels the beauty and makes magic out of the horizontal line, but there is in his work more tenderness, more subtlety, more self-effacement than in Wright's work. It is more refined and has more repose. Perhaps it loses in strength, perhaps it is California that speaks rather than Illinois, any way as work it is, so far as the interiors go, more sympathetic to me.

To create continuity of horizontals in order to effect a homogeneous integrated space composition is a difficult design problem. Even the master, Frank Lloyd Wright, was known to hide staircases because they ruined the horizontality. In the Greenes' designs, the staircases become a *tour de force*, reaffirming the horizontal. They become a prominent element in every house and, as design, are masterpieces..

A continuous horizontal wooden band stretches in every room, embracing disparate elements in an uninterrupted kinetic movement. Derived from the Japanese, it is nonstructural, yet it scales the rooms to human proportions and affirms the structural rhythms of the exterior cage on a reduced scale.

Functional elements—windows and doors— soothe themselves into horizontal configurations rather than asserting themselves into the wall as jarring, vertical cutouts. Extensive use of multiple window and door groupings is made, with sash extending beyond the frames. Doors broadened and lowered in proportion, conform to the horizontal line. French doors provide direct access to patios and open rooms to the outdoors, making of verandas an extension of the room itself. Casement windows open into the room, admitting nature's cooling breath and sunny outpourings but not her showers or drafty whisperings. Nature is admitted into every room as a selective hostess welcomes her guests, with generosity yet reserve.

Most of the bedrooms are adjoined by outdoor porches as beautifully finished as many interior rooms; during the hot summers, occupants could sleep outdoors under a mosquito net, cooled by evening breezes from the heat of the day. Families could sit and be refreshed by rain, have their tea and listen to the talk of rain's life-giving force on the copper drain pipes while remaining dry.

Many elements of English arts and crafts thought were an integral part of every major house the Greenes designed—fireplaces, inglenooks, window seats and private bedrooms. Some of the major homes have a fireplace in every room; each operates well, but is perhaps superfluous because every house also contained a central heating system (some of which are still operating). Many of the houses have semiprivate window seats or inglenooks placed in a darker area of the room, to meet that real human need for a place of intimate proportion in which to be alone and yet within the circle of family. As a child intuitively seeks a hiding place, Charles conceived charming settings for "only a sheltered nook with a cosy seat." Lighting in the houses is a major source of criticism, for it is dim and subdued. Light fixtures hanging from ceilings shed a soft glow in evenings, and lamps, usually art glass or Tiffany pieces, while providing wonderfully warm effects, were ill-suited for reading. It is rather well characterized as religious lighting, which is in keeping with the period and understandable when one remembers the bases of the residential style. A home satisfied man's instinctual and material needs, such as the primeval necessity of shelter, and his spiritual ones as well. The residence existed to serve not only man's rationalized and intellectual needs, but also to symbolize his ideas and his longing for a grasp of the blessed life.

Functionally, the interiors of the major houses divide themselves into three major areas: the formal areas for entertaining, dining and housing guests; the private section for family members to which outsiders rarely, if ever, were admitted; and the functional area, including servants' quarters—which in almost every case were so carefully secluded as to allow the servants to virtually disappear into the woodwork.

The formal area varied according to the needs of the client. Each of the houses except the Pratt house, a winter residence and therefore less formal, has an entry. In the case of the Blacker house, it is on a grand scale with several pieces of furniture designed for it; in the Thorsen house it is rather small, the house being the only one that is set on a plot the size of a city lot. From the entry an orderly and proper progression of spaces took form. Often the entry faced garden or terrace so that an acquaintance might be led directly through the entryway and met there, never gaining admittance to the living room which, while not quite a parlor, was still not an informal gathering place. Rooms rarely adjoined each other and each usually had a sense of entry.

Private family areas were usually confined to upper floors and included not only bedrooms and bath, but also sitting areas and spaces for one to carry out what were considered civilized and cultured pastimes for people of means, such as writing and reading. There was a propriety of spaces, and the family would no more have considered invading the privacy of the functional areas, than the servants would have intruded where they were not supposed to.

Areas for maintenance and service that necessarily issue from the running of a household were separated from the life pattern of the owner. Separate entrances for service people were provided; areas for servants to live, eat and carry out their duties remained remote from the owner's attention. Back stairways from basement to attic were in every house so that neither servant nor owner were embarrassed. Cooking smells, the noise of everyday chores and the sight of tasks, such as washing, ironing and cleaning were isolated from the owner's life.

Implicit to an architectural concept is the molding of the interior spaces and there the Greenes conceived the furnishings as a vital part. They planned each interior as one of a kind, designing custom-made elements for each house, to accord

with its chosen motif. It takes men of considerable artistry to utilize their talents in other forms of expression. Charles was such a man and his expression in the field of interior design was comparable to the finest that Europe was producing in that period. But the Greenes went beyond, designing a home that one could literally move into with simply his clothing and personal belongings. It suggested another sense of order altogether which even Frank Lloyd Wright never carried so far (although he reportedly once bolted his furniture to the floor where he placed it so that the owners could not move it and spoil his architectural concept). The brothers supplied more than exterior shape or shell; they sought to provide an all-conclusive form, an organic unity of intrinsically harmonious elements for an inner and outer life to express itself. A Greene & Greene house required no completion on the owner's part, a sense of order not altogether comfortable to live up to. As an artist, breathing soul and life into his creation, Charles had to complete the aesthetic experience, but no doubt it was mildly disturbing to the owner who in this case not only lived with it, but in it.

Earth colors predominate in Greene interiors, enveloping one in a sense of intimacy much like the tones of a Rembrandt portrait. Materials and colors, blended and chosen for their intrinsic qualities rather than ascribed value, brought both common and expensive elements together. Wood of all kinds found usage, from rare Peruvian mahogany to humble Oregon pine, each expressive of its own character and gift. The various woods have the allure of a flower, seductive with their scent, ravishing the sight with their particular color, pulling the eye beyond the surface to bask in the rich arabesques of the grain patterns. All interior woods breathe life and warmth, rubbed as they were to a furniture finish. Plastered wall areas toned and integrated themselves to the woods. To strike a balance with the subdued, warm tones, oriental rugs with their organically-dyed colors were used, or the brothers designed and had rugs woven to their specifications.

Silver inlay, gilt and semiprecious stones blended with brass and leather in pleasing combinations. The Greenes used art glass, both local and imported, extensively. They designed their own fixtures, using panels of colored glass which they leaded together by a special process—stained glass was never painted—and panels for front doors were molded with the same technique. Grueby, Rookwood, or locally-made Batchelder tiles composed many of their fireplace fronts, reflecting iridescent hues in soft accent. The overall affect of their interiors is first pleasurable, then almost other-worldly, for unpretentious materials become luxurious. All the senses experience involvement. The sight is relaxed by the subtle tonalities of painterly colors, kept alert by momentary splashes of bright, pure colors. The din and noise of everday life is subdued and the sound of wood, as it breathes with the seasons and climate, makes one aware that it is still within the process of life. Real leather and wood smells intoxicate. At every turn, the subtly curved hand-rubbed wooden forms tempt human touch.

For each of the major residences, hand-crafted furniture designed by Charles Greene was custom made; a few houses he furnished totally. Furniture does not exist apart from architecture. Pieces of other eras and modes of life, constructed with pedantic correctness but usually out of scale and concept, invariably moved in with the occupants. The Greenes must have been drawn into designing their own furniture, for like Makintosh, they designed almost solely for the interiors which they created, with no intent to manufacture or mass-produce their designs. Many of the early pieces bear no mark, and it was not until 1912 that Charles registered his trademark, which consisted of his signature, "Sumner Greene," in flowery script with the words, "His True Mark," intertwined, branded into the wood. By the time the U.S. Patent Office officially registered the trademark, the major work had ended.

Until very recently, Greene furniture has been little known, but it stands among the finest that has been produced in America. As C. R. Ashbee noted on his visit to Pasadena,

He [Charles Greene] fetched us in his auto again this afternoon and drove us about, then took us to his workshops where they were making without exception the best and most characteristic furniture I have seen in this country. There were beautiful cabinets and chairs of walnut and lignum-vitae, exquisite dowelling and pegging, and in all a supreme feeling for the material, quite up to the best of our English craftsmanship, Spooner, the Barnslys, Lutyens, Lethaby. I have not felt so at home in any workshop on this side of the Atlantic (but we have forgotten the Atlantic, here it is the Pacific!). Here things were really alive—and the "Arts and Crafts" that all the others were screaming and hustling about, are

actually being produced by a young architect, this quiet, dreamy, nervous, tenacious little man, fighting single-handed until recently against tremendous odds.

If Greene & Greene furniture is a supreme expression of the Arts and Crafts Movement in America, it is because Charles, like Edward Godwin of the English movement, reasserted the importance of the designer over the craftsman. From that position of pre-eminence over the other two necessary members of the triangle—the artisan and workshop owner—nearly all the major developments in furniture have sprung, for it is neither the purpose nor the nature of craftsmanship to initiate and invent. The relationship between designer and maker should not be construed as one of superiority and inferiority, but rather as a division of talents. A designer's ideas are only made possible by skilled craftsmen who can bring them to life. In France, the *ebeniste* often shared his mark with that of the shop from which the piece came.

In Pasadena, John and Peter Hall fulfilled the traditional roles of craftsmen and workshop owners to the designer, Charles Greene. They themselves were both master craftsmen and their company built all the furniture for the Greene brothers' homes. A master furniture and stair maker, as well as wood carver, John Hall presided over much of the construction in the capacity of artisan. Interpreting and translating the sketches, drawn on a scant scale of 1½ inches to one foot, and given the refinements that Charles Greene's furniture entailed, John's talent must have been considerable. Charles' drawings reveal, too, that many changes and alterations took place from the first conceptual image to the final product, though sometimes he would make a prototype of a design, spending his early morning hours at the mill to oversee construction. Invariably, he took tools in hand and worked himself, showing the craftsmen what he had in mind or altering a detail here and there. He had a way about him that engendered both respect and admiration among the men who worked for him. One of his children wrote that because of that special talent, his workers "were always able in some fashion to exceed their limitations."

To the furniture maker belongs the ultimate expression of craft, for his art is the most demanding. Furniture is seen in three dimensions and, because it is movable, from all sides and angles. Other than wall pieces, there are no hidden sides, corners or junctures—there is no place for mistakes

no area to hide shoddy workmanship or an imperfect measurement or method. A joint must be able not only to sustain the stress of considerable weight; it must also be a pleasing connection, or at least unobtrusive. Machines can make initial, intricate cuts for joints but the furniture maker himself must fit the joints with a precision that does not allow for slight miscalculations. Joinery is a telling index of the quality of a piece of furniture and the fineness of a craftsman. Because he used solid woods, Charles Greene's designs utilized an elaborate system of joinery.

English Georgian furniture, the basis of American furniture design, provided a standard from which Charles no doubt started. In turn, English furniture had been greatly influenced by the domestic Chinese pieces that began to appear. Charles Greene found Chinese furniture more than fertile copying ground. He collected, because of his own interest in their qualities of design, domestic pieces of Chinese furniture from the Ming and Ch'ing dynasties, and thus he lived with the source. He tempered the influence of the Orient, translating it into useful occidental forms. In his own home he adapted the Chinese-style bed into a built-in platform.

As do so many items of Greene & Greene design, the furniture suggests an inventive imagination struggling with an almost austere sense of restraint that feared unmeaningful expression. At moments, one sees an almost Shaker-like purity and deceptive simplicity. It was in fact a very costly simplicity, for every piece has an inspired richness contained within its apparently practical form and the simplest design involved a masterly command of line, curve and cubic proportion.

Charles based the scale of furniture upon the scale, not only of the house, but of a particular room. Pieces vary greatly from house to house, subtly from room to room, according to their appointment within the total scheme. In design, the furniture related to the color and motif of the room for which it was made, repeating phrasings of the interior. Square, polished ebony pegs cap screw heads in designed patterning, and joinery, hidden by the Chinese, becomes design as well, exposed and pleasing of form. Black ebony splines lend contrast and dimensionality as well as strength to the structure. As in all Greene & Greene structures, furniture members were rounded with sinuous, ever-so-slight curvatures of chair backs and arms, the result of complex, compounded angles.

Bedroom suites of Greene design could be construed as fittings for the finest stateroom on an Atlantic ocean liner, where everything must be designed for compactness, safety, durability and, of course, some luxury. Pieces display the trimness of fine ship furniture with no sharp edges or protruding parts. Jointed construction allows for expansion and contraction, and wooden handles and pulls are warm to the touch.

Charles designed a variety of tables for every house. A thin, svelte leg with muscular, steel-like strength, prevailed and table tops and shelves had cleated edges. For dining room tables, Charles used a large plank of solid lignum-vitae, a hard, heavy wood of luxurious smoothness that possesses a self-lubricating quality which makes it impervious to cracks. Tabletops usually had wide overhangs with rounded, cleated edges, often relieved with ebony splines or pegs. The top rested upon a heavy base centered in the middle of the table rather than on a confusion of pudgy legs, creating the feeling of a thin, graceful horizontal slab, divorced from any visible means of support. Reminiscent of the Shaker sense of simple functionalism, the tables defy covering and are a superb statement of purpose.

Built-in pieces demonstrated the same precision and perfection as pieces seen in dimensionality. Charles used the finest cabinet woods available for his wardrobes, bookcases and chests. He expended thoughtful consideration on extra features, such as adjustable bookcase shelves to accommodate any size book, and in some cases tiny hand-crafted keys for bookcase doors.

A standard bedroom suite included beds, usually single, with a bed table, a man's dresser or chiffonier, a low dressing table with a mirror and dressing stools for the lady, a writing desk, sitting chairs, and usually a rocking chair. In style, the chests are reminiscent of the Oriental *tansu* chest, with Charles showing geometrical ingenuity in his asymmetrical placement of drawers within the symmetrical confines of the chest. Charles' chests exhibit originality and variety. Drawers are jointed and beautifully finished, inside and out. Every drawer runs on a notched center guide so that the heaviest drawer opens with the pull of one hand.

Handles of wood mold themselves to the fingertips.

A writing desk is found in every bedroom; for women of that period, letter writing was an important and cultured form of expression. Each desk contained fitted compartments for all the writing necessities, including a small drawer for stamps, covered by a drop front. Arm supports of wood slid out automatically as the front was lowered. When not in use, the desk presented a handsome facade.

The Japanese decorative influence appears in Charles' use of inlay. A four-legged piece of furniture by nature is symmetrical, so Charles provided counterpoint to the symmetry of many pieces with asymmetrical, lyrical designs done in inlay. His patterns derived from the organic world, sensuous and bending floral motifs with *art nouveau* implications. They revolved around abstract wood grain patterns, carefully chosen for their design and enriched with mother-of-pearl, ribbons of silver, and semiprecious stones. His inlay work is quite unique in this respect and gracefully delicate in contrast to the geometry of drawers and legs. It adds both beauty and a sense of scale.

THE RESIDENTIAL STYLE
The Outstanding Commissions

Designed generally with a span of a few years, the eight homes described in the following pages embody the finest conceptions of Greene & Greene and are among the most complete architectural statements. They by no means comprise all the large and fine residences that the brothers built, but they do express the general principles by which Greene & Greene can be known, and they epitomize the values of the American residential style.

In 1902, James A. Culbertson commissioned the firm to build a sizeable residence for him. The home which the brothers designed was the first of three major framed-timber houses, each a variation of that style. They reveal a progression of influences, the first having been built almost immediately after Charles' return from England, with the English Tudor still fresh in his mind. The other two followed the Bandini bungalow, previously discussed, and drew upon the experience gained from having built many bungalows, the Tichenor house in 1905, and the house for Henry Robinson in 1906.

In appearance and setting the James Culbertson residence is the most reminiscent of the English country house. In its covering of long shakes, the house, situated on a corner site, blends with the surrounding gardens and greenery.

Massing was along traditional lines, with a basic rectangular form as central, but the Greenes handled even traditional mass forms with originality. In this house, which the Greenes later remodeled, the predominant feeling is of a Tudor country home with its steeply-pitched roof and twin gables, a roof form which the Greenes adapted and used in later houses. Overhanging eaves made their appearance, but not until later, as in the Robinson house, do they assume their characteristically long Greene & Greene outreach. Casement windows, reminiscent of the Swiss chalet, were introduced but the most

striking windows are two oriels on the face of the house, composed of small, diamond-shaped panes in the English manner.

The architects used exposed masonry extensively in both the Culbertson and Tichenor houses, with the Robinson house much less endowed. A low, rambling wall surrounds and delineates the Culbertson property, and walkways of blended bricks and fieldstones grace the land around the home. On the Tichenor grounds, a wall proceeding from the ends of the house around to the street front, is composed of clinkers resting on mammoth rocks, with heaps of the bricks massed on the tops of the entry posts. Integrating bulky, gray cobblestones with clinker bricks may have been an invention of Charles' artistic eye, but the use of clinker bricks themselves certainly was not. In England, houses built entirely of burnt bricks and clinkers, such as the well-known farmhouse of Samuel Collett, built in 1820, were thought to be the ultimate in picturesqueness, and the shaggy facades, if a bit rough, seemed to blend the house into the countryside. The frame of the entire ground floor of the Tichenor house is filled with clinker bricks; the framing itself comes closest to the feeling of the medieval half-frame with the wooden members joined by pegs.

At the same time, the Greenes blended decorative Oriental elements into the Tichenor design. A tile roof covers the structure and Chinese ceramic tiles of green were prominently designed into the garden gates. Enfolded within the wings of the house stands a Japanese-style garden with a teahouse and a small arched bridge over a stream.

In exterior view, the Robinson House appears as the most characteristic of the half-timber houses as Americans know them. Constructed of stucco-covered brick, the half-timber structure predominates, particularly in the second story. Traditional

crux forms stand out clearly. Though extraneous structurally, they were deliberately designed into the structure to impart that sense of vitality and life which medieval forms suggested. Capping the frame, the roof, however, assumes the lowered profile and pitch that the Greenes evolved. It is composed of roofing paper, rather than of shakes, with edges rolled to create continuity of line.

The Greenes devised unique shaded outdoor areas and pergolas for each of these homes. At the front of the Culbertson house, a carved pergola extends from the porch to a round, covered arbor, and a carved trellis composed of handsomely bowed crosspieces with rounded beam ends resting on elliptical redwood purlins, casts softened shadows along one edge of the property.

In the Tichenor house, a pergola stretches nearly the entire length of one wing and a gazebo, a favorite Victorian structure, creates a backdrop for the extensive planting around the house. The Greenes expanded the Robinson house living room with a large pergola and upstairs a balcony provides a shaded area for day and a sleeping area for summer nights.

In both the Tichenor and Robinson houses, the Japanese practice of orienting the living rooms away from the street was adopted. Each house commanded an extraordinary view—the Tichenor house, located in Long Beach, overlooks the ocean and the Robinson house was set high on a bluff overlooking the Arroyo Seco in Pasadena. In plan, the Tichenor house revolves around a two-story massing of near rectangular form facing the sea. Two low wings of the first story extend out, one from each end, equal neither in length nor width, thus assigning an asymmetrical quality to an otherwise simple plan. The slender east wing advances beyond the front of the house in counterbalance to the heavier, wider stance of the west wing. Sheltered within the wings lies the courtyard with a Japanese garden, shielded from street view. Several entries open into the house, the main one on the ocean-front, where banks of square-paned French windows expose nearly the entire facade to the ocean view. Another entrance of lesser size on the west side of the house opens into an entry hall where the stairway leads to the second story.

On the second floor, a gallery, sheltered by overhanging eaves, extends the length of the front and west elevation, reminiscent of a widow's walk. French doors allow access or shelter to view the sea.

The Robinson house is comprised of large, spacious rooms which revolve around a sizable entry hall which, as the central circulating core of the house, eliminates dark awkward hallways and useless space. As mentioned, the plan orients itself to the back of the site where a vista of several miles up and down the arroyo could be scanned from the living room, dining room and open loggia. The second story repeats the intention with each of three large bedrooms facing an uninterrupted view of the arroyo. A clever placement of the service area made it a quite separate entity from the house, thus isolating the service functions from the living areas and the owners' attention. The Greenes angled this wing asymmetrically to the front wall of the house, thereby preventing a sprawl across the width of the lot while at the same time placing the domestic help within close accessibility. More than merely practical, such a placement added interest to the plan.

In interior concept, the same evolving of influences reveals itself, beginning with England and progressing to the Orient. The Culbertson house took its main inspiration from the English Arts and Crafts Movement. Such materials as quarter-sawed oak and stained art glass compose the entry and stairway, reminiscent of Morris, yet Greene & Greene in execution. The opalescent glass panels of the front door depict a country scene with an English-style cottage, and carved oak panels stand on either side of the door. Throughout the interior are handsome, hand-carved patterns in wood—Charles' talent and love for wood carving is nowhere more abundantly or beautifully evident. The most strikingly unique work embellishes the dining room, where the influence of the rage for Japonica, extant in England, expressed itself. Scenes carved in low relief, reminiscent of a woodcut of Mount Fuji, stand above the fireplace depicting cloud-shrouded mountains. Redwood panels above and

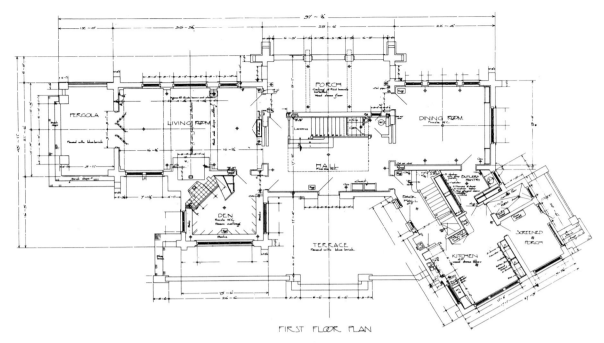

Residence for Henry M. Robinson, Pasadena, 1906.

around the room pick up and repeat the cloud theme, as does the metal fireplace hood below. What would have seemed a ponderously heavy room with paneled walls and a ceiling of redwood becomes an atmospheric chamber with an ethereal quality. In the living room, a long shallow window seat is banked with leaded casement windows that look upon the garden.

In the Tichenor interior, the Greenes began to interweave their influences, with the Oriental becoming pleasurable decoration. Furniture drawings express arts and crafts concepts, with chairs reminiscent of Morrisonian straightforwardness and even a "Morris chair" design *per se* included. A desk was designed with batten doors, and tables conform to the standard arts and crafts placement of legs. Joinery and pegging, prominent aspects of design, suggest the crafted look and no inlay is found. In material, a handsome screen with leather panels seems molded in the English tradition, yet, at the same time, the Greenes' ingenious adaptation of Ming-inspired design elements appears in all the furniture. Chinese-style bracketing underscores the chair seats, and the lift pattern, a typical motif in Chinese domestic furniture, begins to make its notable contribution to Greene & Greene pieces.

Leaded-glass windows in the dining room meld both influences, depicting the theme of birds in flight. Finally, a doorplate of metal, designed by the Greenes, depicts an owl, symbol, in the mind of man, of intelligence and the otherworldly.

The most striking and dramatic feature of the Robinson house interior is the entry which soars upward two stories in a sweeping, spatial *tour de force*. This open well frees the interior space and eliminates a closed-box treatment of the first and second stories. A balcony on the second floor, visible from the first, overlooks the large entry. A six-sided lantern, suspended on chains, descends from the ceiling of the second floor to the lower, creating one large volume and unifying the two floors as one entity.

In contrast to the medieval half-timber concept embodied in the exterior, the feeling of the interior is decidedly Oriental. The entry diffuses such a sense of ordered harmony and pleasing tonalities that one can envision a mandarin of Peking finding it quite compatible with his sense of beauty.

Paneled in cedar, in board and batten pattern, the wooden entry displays the elegance of fine furniture finish. The stairwell is exposed, a bold series of horizontal bands against the vertical battens; their horizontally is echoed in wooden bands which accent the wall battens. A diagonal railing joins the two elements into harmonious confluence with sweeping abstractions. Opposite the stairwell, a bank of windows on the second floor filters the sunlight that fall upon the entire form, indirectly illuminating the lower hall as well. Chinese chairs of Ming origin stand in the hall, chosen by Charles not only for their architectural contribution to the scheme, but for the tone of quiet dignity and order they lend in rarefied manner. Again, the words of Cram seem apropos as he described the Greenes' work: ". . . there are things in it Japanese; things that are Scandinavian; things that hint of Sikkim, Bhutan, and the fastness of Tibet."

The living room is paneled in dark Peruvian mahogany, a richly-toned wood of deep-hued elegance, with every corner carved. Corners reach outward in both directions with petal-like forms in carved undulant patterns that dissolve finally into elongated forms along the panels. They heighten the sense of dimensionality and structure. The furniture designed for the room reveals Ming-inspired elements; in particular, a couch suggests the influence of Chinese domestic furniture in its simplicity and elegance of modeling, and a mirror designed to fit in the wall paneling, seems to be an inspired translation of a Chinese yoke rack. In the dining room, chairbacks repeat Ming subtleties of curve. Above the dining room table hovers a very large fixture with a stylized cherry tree pattern in art glass, shedding a soft amber glow over the entire table.

From the richly-appointed living area, the Greenes made a quiet detour to common materials in the den with charm and success. An angled wall of soft brown brick (*Craftsman* magazine commented that it was surprising to see how finished an effect could be given to a material supposedly adapted to exterior use) contains a small fireplace. An inglenook was composed around the fireplace by angling from the wall a bench of fumed oak, carved and constructed with butterfly joints. Metal work in black iron, including a simple wrought iron hood shielding the fireplace and fixtures, stands in striking contrast to the soft hue of the room. Pale amber leaded glass accents the soft browns and yellows of the other furnishings and sheds subdued light on the bookshelves lining the three walls.

The *Craftsman* magazine wrote of the Robinson house: "It would be difficult to imagine a house more characteristic of this Western state, for it holds the spirit of both the old life and the new, is picturesque from every angle and at the same time is obviously designed for the convenience and contentment of the owners. A home of this type is more than an individual dwelling place; it is a permanent monument of the life of the people and the period."

Although the Greene brothers were known primarily for their wooden houses, they also constructed some houses of plaster exterior. As well as the plaster complement of the half-timber framed house for Mrs. Robinson, the brothers executed two other major commissions in cement-based materials. Drawings for a house of stucco exterior for Mrs. Freeman Ford were begun shortly after those for her sister, Mrs. L. A. Robinson, next door, and one of their last major commissions, a residence for the Culbertson sisters, displayed an exterior of gunite, a fine cement applied with an air gun.

The Greenes had respect for material, whatever it might be, and they utilized plaster, as they did wood, as an end in itself. Charles did have strong feelings about plaster-finished exteriors, but they did not stem from a dislike for the material, as some have supposed. "Just a word of protest against the use of blinding white paint and plaster. It may be excusable in a dull country where the sun never shines in all its splendor, but here in California, we should have some pity for tired eyes . . . it is inconceivable that we should be so unfeeling or careless as to neglect . . . color. Appropriate color should be the aim, but most certainly color." Needless to say, the Greenes tinted their plaster exteriors to earthen tones, close to terra-cotta in color, investing the finish with the vitality of stone and the texture of fine sand.

In plan, the Freeman Ford residence is a patio house, the earlier Bandini court now brought to full development and expression. In this conception, the patio became an entrance court, with the rooms arranged around it but not opening into it. Quarters for the domestic help constitute one wing and the family's private quarters the other. The living areas orient themselves away from the patio at the back of the house, since the Ford house stands next to the Robinson house on the bluff above the arroyo and has the advantage of the same superb view. This adaptation of the patio plan responded to the sense of privacy that Americans demanded. Bedrooms in the family wing adjoin and lead through to each other, as they do in the Bandini plan, but they also connect to an outer hall which parallels the court. Unique to the plan stand two second-story rooms

one rising above the entry and the other perched like a separate little cottage above a bedroom with its own side entrance on the south court. Each of these rooms has bands of windows, like lookout towers, and they add both interest and elevation to the plan. Facing the arroyo, the dining room bank of windows affords an expansive view.

Set a good distance back on the site, the house cannot be seen from the street. A lantern, perched at the entrance to the patio court, provides a focal point as one approaches the house via a curving driveway. A set of steps lead from the driveway to the formalized patio through an ivy-covered pergola, which delineates the court and composes an architectural completion of the house. Entry to the house lies across the tile-paved patio court and around a sunken square, planted in a formal manner with a small lily pool. The gracious progression from the busy street to the quiet of a friend's home reveals the sensitivity of the Greene & Greene touch.

Overhanging beams shadow the tinted stucco exterior, crowned by a roof of characteristic low pitch, composed of roofing paper rolled over the edge for a smoothness of line. The overhang of the roof shelters long, crafted benches of Greene design.

Many of the materials found in the interior of the Freeman Ford house the Greenes also used in the Robinson house, though differently in both form and feeling. The entry is of cedar, but stained to a darker tone than in the Robinson house. In the living room, a long low fireplace of pressed brick is composed into patterns that utilize every dimension and shape of brick in thick and thin designs, in receding and advancing forms. Hand-crafted batten doors of twice the usual door-width exist throughout the interior, with screw heads placed in patterned design. Wooden locks, too, become part of the design and they open and shut with pleasing clicks even today. In this house, the Greenes made elegant use of art glass in door panels and windows. Molded into a peacock theme, the design is among the most sensuous and luminous found in their houses. Fixtures are set flush with the ceiling, an unusual treatment of light-source in the early 1900s.

A writer of the time described the Freeman Ford house as an "adaptation of the best he [the architect] has found in Switzerland, in Italy and in Japan, and the courtyard reminds us of all three of his favorite store houses. It is another example of the successful California patio, open to the east, paved, with intensive planting, and with a charm all its own."

This page, and opposite: *House for Mr. R. R. Blacker, Pasadena, 1907. (Estate subdivided and furnishings auctioned upon death of Mrs. Blacker. Excellently maintained by present owners.)*

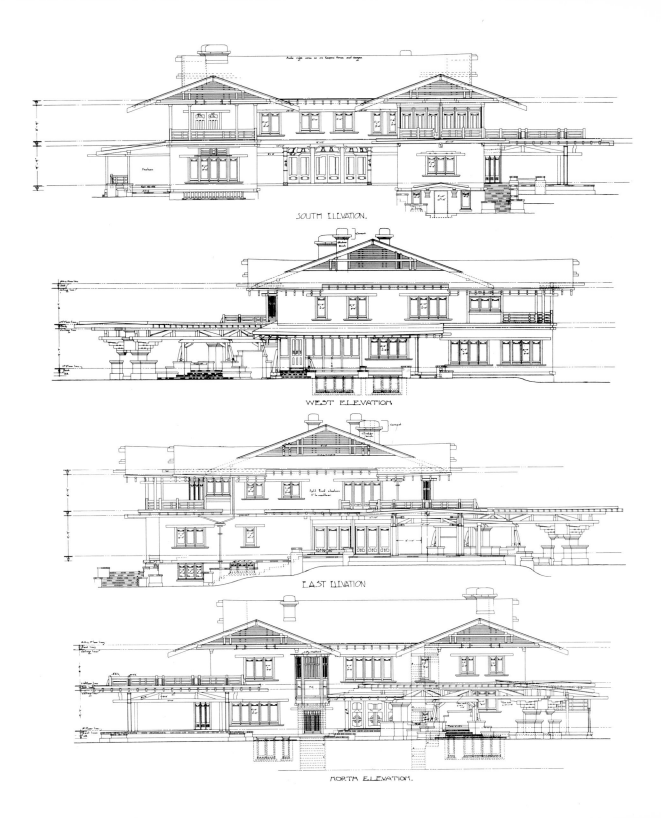

SOUTH ELEVATION.

WEST ELEVATION

EAST ELEVATION

NORTH ELEVATION.

Below: *Blacker house; favrile glass lantern in the living hall.*

To categorize a residence of approximately 9,000 square feet as a bungalow seems a contradiction in terms, yet that is exactly what the house for Mr. R. R. Blacker is—a picturesque bungalow on a grand scale. Covered with shingles, considered a common and homely material, and set unobtrusively within the landscape, the Blacker House is nothing other than a bungalow, *par excellence*. It stands firmly within the domestic wooden tradition that sought antimonumentalism both in materials and techniques. The biggest surprise, however, is the richly appointed and expensive interior within this picturesque shell, for the bungalow was generally thought of as an impermanent, inexpensive style.

In 1907, the original plan for the R. R. Blacker house was drawn up by the office of Myron Hunt and Elmer Gray, one of the foremost firms in Southern California, and published. The plan revealed an H-shaped manor house with the exterior clad in mission-style stucco. While the Blackers were people of considerable means and wanted a house of refinement, they ostensibly sought something less plain and more picturesque. When Mr. Blacker purportedly saw the "Swiss village" of Greene design on Arroyo Terrace, he substituted the firm of Greene & Greene as his architects, while retaining the basic plan of the Hunt-Gray office. Undoubtedly, the rather informal character of the California bungalow, as it was then widely known, was the Blackers' preference, for that is precisely what the Greenes delivered—a rather traditional plan clothed in bungalow fashion. And they did it superbly.

Blacker house; approach to front entrance through porte-cochere.

The site for the Blacker house lay in the Oak Knoll district which an early writer for the *Pasadena Daily News* described as "our only remaining Pasadena reminder of the old oak forest which once covered the entire upper valley." A large corner site was the chosen place, raised as it was above adjoining streets. Upon this choice site, the Greenes created a magical summertime world, similar in feeling to the painted one of the Impressionists. They designed, constructed and furnished a main house for Mr. and Mrs. Blacker, a garage with living quarters, a keeper's cottage, a lath house for plants, a little summer house and shady pergolas. They surrounded their structures with a painterly landscape that embraced a large, free-form lotus pool fed by a trickling stream, a vegetable garden, and sentinel trees and plants. Stepping-stone paths and walkways, following the roll of the terrain and the dip of knolls and dells, loosely tie the land to the house. Within that scheme, the house rests on a knoll that commands a view of the San Gabriel Mountains to the north and smiles upon a specially-created world in every other direction.

Although based on a traditional H-shaped plan, the Blacker house evolved into a free, asymmetrical composition as the Greenes developed it. They extended the front wing with a covered terrace, wider than the adjoining living room and reaching from the side of the house to beyond the front. From this covered terrace, a view of the Japanese garden and lotus pond comes into vision and beyond stands the panorama of the lower San Gabriel valley. In counterbalance, the opposite end of the H was extended by an architectural pergola that stretches from the dining area. Roofed with delicate wisteria blossoms, the pergola, when in bloom, casts a mandle of lavender over the glass porch and shelters a seat at the opposite end. In graceful counterpoint, a small irregular-shaped terrace flanks the rear of the other wing. The symmetry of the H-plan is most dramatically countered, however, by the angled placement of a massive porte-cochere to the straight wall of entry. Supported by trusses and a stepped pylon, the imposing structure spans the distance from the entry to the lawn, sheltering a circular driveway that curves from the street. Entry through the porte-cochere provides an indirect approach, intimate yet impressive, making the house an expectation and something quite apart from the usual.

An entry hall, grand both in scale and concept, is the spatial center of the house. It performs the same function as the large central living hall that Richardson had made a significant part of domestic planning, though without a fireplace. Here the hall becomes the pivotal center, from which the dining and living areas are axially disposed in minimal segmentation. To this oversized pivot, spaces freely adjust themselves to function and expression: largesse without pretense.

As in Richardson's great living halls, a large area is given to the stairwell which expands the vertical space even as the hall itself liberates the horizontal movement. For this living area, the Greenes designed several sizeable pieces of furniture and thus it functions as an open and informal main living area as well as a horizontal-vertical circulation core. It unfolds to a court through French doors directly opposite the entrance. To the right is the dining wing, segmented by a sectional glass wall that detaches the breakfast sunporch from the dining room. It dissolves into folds to make one large room when occasion requires. The more formal, seclusive living room is to the left.

In like arrangement, the upstairs disposes itself into a few large areas, consisting of two bedroom suites and hidden quarters for the domestics. One suite includes a bedroom with a sitting room, bath and outdoor balcony. The master bedroom suite consumes the entire left leg of the H, and is composed of a substantial bedroom, a dressing room, bath and a sunroom overlooking a balcony. An interesting aspect of the plan is the placement of a billiard room in the basement. Situated in a hollow that faces the garden, the room sits above grade and has its own outside entrance, as well as private access from the main entry.

Framed in Oregon pine, the two-story structure rests on a clinker brick foundation set with darkened mortar. Exposed structural members were hand-cleaned with a wire brush to enhance textural interest, and, as in all their work, rounded beam ends, formed by hand-labor, support the structural sense. To find suitable beams for this oversized bungalow, special buying trips were made to Northern California lumber yards. Split redwood shakes, dipped in a mellow, brown-green stain, furnish a rough texture effect that brings the house into affinity with the russet and gold of the land.

Structural expressionism reached its most sophisticated and refined level in the Blacker House, both in interior and exterior execution. Corbelling is used in unusual and unexpected places, reinforcing both structure and the sense thereof. Dowels join

Blacker house; view of front entrance from living hall of Burmese teak.

Blacker house.
Above: *Door detail.*
Opposite: *South veranda.*

structural members together in enriching patterns. Cold, gray steel straps, held firm by driven wedges, clamp beams together in bold patterned abstraction. Buttresses, used as architectural supports, insinuate crux forms with tree-like strength, dramatizing the sense of support. Here and there, walls dissolve into structural entities, with one story divorced both in material and structure from the plane above or below. French doors break from the wall plane into a V onto the east terrace and from the sunroom to the balcony on the second floor. Mortised beam ends reach beyond each other and emphasize the thrust outward. Window sills and header beams extend beyond window frames, and railings echo the horizontal line, dissolving the wall as monolithic facade.

A gabled roof, apropos to the manor house plan, ventilates the structure perfectly, even the second story. Composed of the same textured shakes that paint the frame, the roof is pitched low, a flattened version of its English progenitor. Balcony roofs extend beneath the gables in splayed hand-spreads, covered with composition sheet roofing.

The articulation of structural elements finds boundless expression. Gutters and drainpipes achieve abstraction rather than distraction in the angular forms as contrived by the Greenes. Foundation vents, even exposed mudsills, express design.

The Blacker house is the focal point around which the Greenes created their impressionistic world of tamed nature. Similar to the villa concept, the grounds are an architectural extension of the house, planned both in sympathy to and enrichment of the natural terrain. From the east terrace, the capacious lotus pool nourished by a trickling stream and a small waterfall comes into view, its irregular shape punctuated by carefully placed stones. A rhythmic flow of pathways, composed of rocks and stepping stones rather than solid materials, seductively beckons the wanderer among the gardens. Following their lead the picturesque buildings slowly reveal themselves and the contrived turns and curves provide a sense of surprise and discovery, a highly cultivated effect of Japanese gardens. At the far end of the pool stands the summer house, a place to contemplate and a focal point from the living room. The south court opposite the entry overlooks a protected garden which embraces a sunken, circular bird bath.

The interior of the Blacker house, elaborate and luxurious, dispels the notion of a picturesque informal residence. The first impression upon entering is of the grandness of scale and elegance of

Blacker house.
Above: *South elevation with outdoor entrance to basement billiard room; sunroom and deck of master bedroom above.*
Right: *Detail of rafters and lantern, taken from east elevation.*

Blacker house.
Above: *Staircase.* Above right: *Detail of stair rail.*
Right: *Stair lantern.*
Opposite page: *Oriel overlooking the landing.*

appointment. A low, wide batten door, which integrates panels of iridescent art glass in floral patterns, opens into an intimate entry, formed by the corbelled beams of the stair landing above. From this subdued beginning, the living hall bursts into height, setting the stage for discovery and flights of fancy. Composed in teak of golden luster, with several pieces of furniture to augment the scale, the entry sets the tone of the gracious yet unostentatious refinement and artistic expression found throughout the house.

This hall is composed of an incredible multiplicity of parts resolved into one harmonic entity of overwhelming beauty. The ceiling is beamed in teak with battened panels running perpendicular to the beams. Lanterns with floral-patterned art glass hang in graceful counterpoint to the geometry of the ceiling. Banks of French doors shed southern light upon the entire room, dispelling what could have been a somber, heavy mood; suffused with light, the hand-rubbed teak members shed a golden bloom.

Among the most imposing structures of Greene design is the oversized stairway in this house. It flows into the entry like a cascading waterfall, with an undulating wave pattern rounding each stair to modulate vertical thrust. Stair planks tumble one beyond the other in corbelled structure, the horizontal lines emphasized by wooden squared pegs. Overlapping box joints add dimensionality and design. Every structural member expresses its own identity and integrity within the whole, yet transcends its role, as a view of the end posts eloquently reveals. Presiding over the stair landing is an oriel window that shelters a window seat. In the lower half, an intricate lattice pattern encircles clusters of glass grapes in luxuriant tones of purple; the upper half is composed of smaller windows that open. A lantern, suspended from the second-story ceiling lifts the eyes to the second floor, to wander over the landing and the railing. Only panels of solid wood were used, never veener. The grain of wide planks changes its spectrum from dark to light with shifting daylight. A storage wall of matching panels carries the continuity, concealing a door of entry to the domestic staff's quarters. Exposed beams stretch across the second-story ceiling and extend from the interior beyond the exterior roof line.

From the yellow-brown hues of the entry, the Greenes shifted tone and feeling in the living room. It is as if the room were a recreation of the natural landscape beyond its windows, the very elements plucked from the realistic world and transformed

Blacker house; linen press in upper hall. Second door from left conceals entrance to quarters of domestic help.

Blacker house; detail of wall in sun room, part of master bedroom suite.

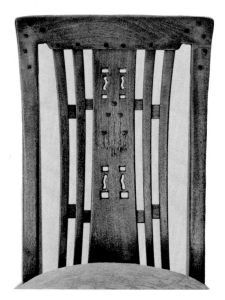

Blacker house furniture.
Opposite page, left: *Entry bench of teak with chest built into seat.* Center: *Living-room rocking chair upholstered with brocade.* Right: *Dining-room chair of mahogany, with polished horse-hide leather seat.*

Above, left: *Entry piece with teak door, carved by Charles Greene; tree form composes handle.* Center: *Living-room straight-back chair with ebony splines and lotus stem design.* Right: *Dining-room chair; detail of back inlaid with mother-of-pearl.*

into transcendental symbols. Paneled in a hardwood of dark hue, this room gives forth an aura of spirituality, its otherworldly colors and materials bringing to mind the paintings of Klimt.

The essence of the room emanates from a gold-leaf ceiling; as background it possesses the dual quality of a plane and of infinite otherworldly noncolor, becomes both a golden reflecting pool, shedding iridescent glimmer over the room, and a fathomless deep. It spills from the ceiling to the panels above the room banding in which raised lotus patterns anchor themselves.

Antique Persian rugs translate nature into arabesques of flower and foliage on a background of muted blue. Rookwood facing tiles on the fireplace pick up the tones of the rug in glazes of chameleon iridescence, and each of six lanterns suspended from the ceiling paraphrase the floral motif in art glass

designs, in color accent to the rug. Octagonal at the base, with splines that open outward like flower petals, the lanterns shed light that flickers like a thousand candles on the golden ceiling.

In itself the room is heavy and dark, laden as it is with so many rich materials and deep-toned elements. Like an Italian painting, it requires the created landscape—lotus pool, gardens, expanse of lawn and trees—to complete it, with the summer-house a fulcrum between the living room and the infinite vista beyond.

The Greene brothers furnished the house completely with exquisitely refined pieces designed to complement the architectural scale of the house. Living room furniture carries out the Oriental flavor, with chairs upholstered in Chinese brocade material and a delicate floral inlay pattern tracing the curve of the chair backs. A desk with a removable top

that doubles as a chest is particularly unusual. In the entry, a long bench with storage beneath the seats stands on carved feet in a Chinese scroll pattern. The Greenes complemented it with heavy upholstered chairs with Morris backs.

For the dining room and breakfast porch, tables and chairs are matched sets so that when the sectional glass wall is folded back, the two sets can be joined together, along with the room. A rectangular fixture, suspended on leather straps, sheds light on both the dining table and the ceiling.

Bedroom furnishings for the Blacker house are among the most handsome bedroom pieces Charles designed. A piece of particular beauty is a cabinet designed for the master bedroom. Reminiscent again of a Ming piece, it has two sets of drawers on each side of a tall center cabinet, supported on muscular legs of unusual slenderness.

57

NORTH ELEVATION

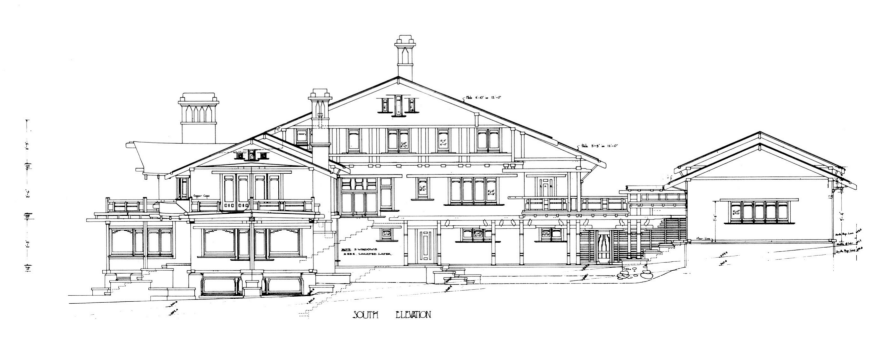

SOUTH ELEVATION

William R. Thorsen house, Berkeley, 1908.
(Presently owned by fraternity.)

WEST ELEVATION

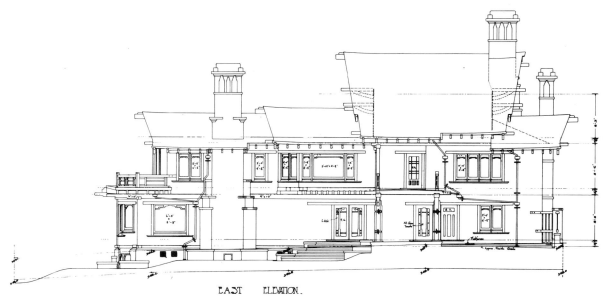

EAST ELEVATION.

Upon near-completion of the Blacker House, the Greene brothers launched construction of the Gamble House, described in the following chapter. When the David B. Gamble house was finished in February, 1909, the firm began work on plans for two more large commissions nearly simultaneously; one for Mrs. Blacker's sister, Mrs. William R. Thorsen, the other for her college roommate at Vassar, Mrs. Pratt.

Mrs. Thorsen imported the brothers to Berkeley, a city already noted for many fine architects of that period, such as Bernard Maybeck and John Galen Howard. Mrs. Pratt then coaxed the brothers even farther north to build a home in Ojai.

Situated in the Berkeley Hills, the Thorsen house is one of the few major residential houses that the Greenes built on a city lot. It resembles a town house, occupying almost the entire lot with little surrounding land. The site, however, basked in a breathtaking view of the San Francisco Bay and the ocean; on a very clear day, the Farallon Islands, more than 25 miles out to sea, stand in view.

In atmosphere, the Thorsen house interior is like the grand salon of a great ship. In that, the Greenes may have been inspired by the pages of *Studio International* and other art publications; these were filled with pictures of elegant ship interiors that the finest artisans and most famous designers of Europe were employed to create. The house seems surprisingly intimate, considering that it contained eight bedrooms as well as servants' quarters, but there is a shipshape quality and sense of fitness that sustains the closeness and intimacy of feeling.

The large rectangular living room is climaxed at one end in a V, like the prow of a ship, and a redwood beam, the bowsprit, extends from the interior through the V to the outside. Teak predominates, crafted like the fittings of a yacht, with mortise and tenon joints covered with square pegs, and the Greene vocabulary of joinery, bracketing and pegging. Built-in furnishing and fixtures are secured throughout the house. Long bookcases with glass doors and adjustable shelves arrange themselves along the length of the living room and a built-in desk and numerous sets of drawers sequester themselves into the paneling. In the dining room, a hanging dish closet fits snugly to the wall and, in the subdued entry, a mirror is set flush into the fully paneled walls. Fixtures, too, are flush to the ceiling. At the end of the hall which joins the living areas, a large painting of a shipwreck,

59

Thorsen house.
Right: *Detail of entry with lilac design in art glass.*
Below: *Fireplace screen of repousse white metal. Chair
back inlaid with mother-of-pearl.*

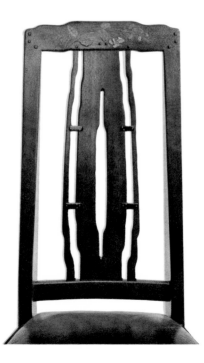

mounted in a frame done by the Greenes, is slant-set from the wall.

L-shaped in plan, the leg of the L looks to the sea and comprises the living room, dining room, den, and a narrow entry, all made subordinate to the view. Even so, the small entry quiets the din of the street and provides that moment of transition. Though situated near the front of the lot, the stained-glass entrance door is approached indirectly via semicircular stairs entered from either side. Structurally, the Thorsen house presents an ample, but not imposing facade.

Exterior walls are shingled in stained, textured shakes and the foundation of dark maroon clinkers and bricks settles the house into sympathetic conformity with the slope of the hillside. Heavy timber sills, mortised together with ends that extend at the corners, station the house firmly upon the foundation. A gabled roof covers the structure and shelters several balconies, repeating the basic Greene form in its low pitch and overhanging eaves, but modified in accent to the atmospheric moods of the Bay area. With frequently changing skies, often filled with rolling clouds and storms from the sea, the balcony roofs have copper coverings to welcome the sounds of the rain; eaves are cut back over the picture window in the living room and from the front of the house for a panoramic view of nature's stirrings. A covered balcony, too, joins the garage to the house, sheltering both terrace and traveler from the rain.

Though the house presumes upon most of the site, the architects made space for an enclosed garden with trellised arcades and a pergola with seats. Here, the Greenes may be said to have truly landscaped the house with the atmosphere.

A particularly striking exterior feature is the beautifully-detailed iron work—perhaps the shrouds of fog that so often envelop the Bay region inspired such strong statements. Reminiscent of Makintosh in design, wrought iron railings and arch-shaped lantern supports, adorning the entry gates, make bold geometricized patterns. The gates themselves embody a shipwreck scene within the overall design, setting the tone for the seaworthy nature of this house.

Mr. and Mrs. Charles M. Pratt made their home in New Jersey but, as did many wealthy Easterners, wintered in California. They preferred Ojai, a fertile valley nestled among mountains and situated inland from the coast, similar to Pasadena, and by then rivalling it as a fashionable resort and exclusive wintering spa. Mrs. Pratt commissioned the Greenes to design a winter home to be built on a ridge of land that tumbled into a thickly-grown canyon and overlooked a sweeping view of the Ojai valley.

A symbiotic relationship exists between the landscape and the Pratt house, the house seemingly spawned from the surrounding land. The gentle slope of the hilly terrain is translated into gabled roofs spread wide and pitched low; the texture of live oak and the thicket lives in the shakes that sheath the exterior. The stuff of existence, stone, becomes wall and chimney cover, stepping-stone, pathway and post support. Long-fingered rafter splines have copper covers to protect the beam ends, now weathered to a patina like the green of the shrub-covered hills. Splayed roofs of trapezoidal shape reach out of the hills and cover terraces and sleeping porches edged with wooden railings.

Charles M. Pratt residence, Ojai, 1909.

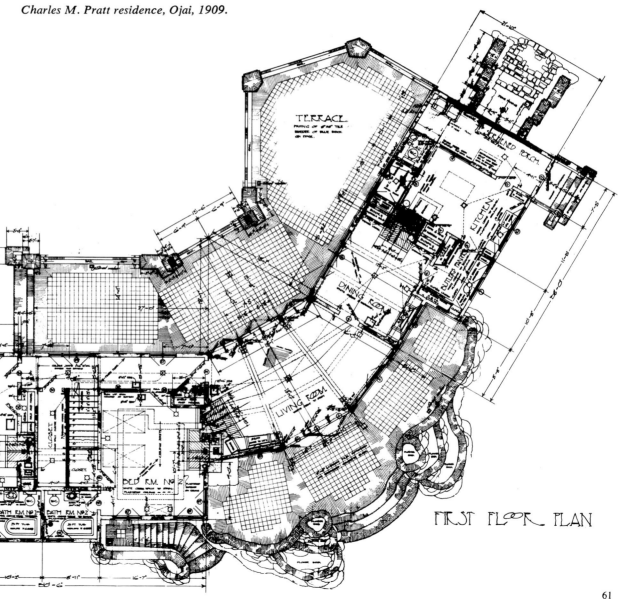

FIRST FLOOR PLAN

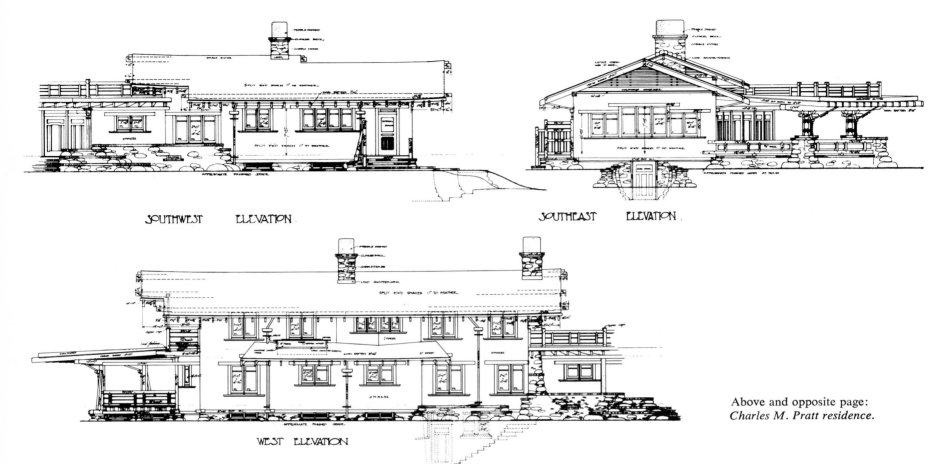

SOUTHWEST ELEVATION.

SOUTHEAST ELEVATION.

WEST ELEVATION

Above and opposite page:
Charles M. Pratt residence.

Hidden from the road, the house is found at the end of a driveway that follows an ambling, indirect path much like a hiker, with lanterns as guides. A terrace, circumscribed by clinker-brick retaining walls resting on large boulders, surrounds the house entry with three tiers for flower beds, formed by serpentine-shaped walls, embracing the curved entry stairs.

For the plan, the Greenes took their cue from the land, bending the shape in a crescent around the rim of the site. The house is but a single room deep, with a second story over one wing only, but the total living space is nearly doubled by the outdoor terraces and verandas that surround the mass. Entry is directly into the trapezoidal-shaped living room, a plan that suits the informality of the house. Opposite the entrance, a wall of French doors dissolves into a veranda with terraces on either side.

The living room composes itself as the central core from which the crescent plan emanates. Because of this unusual form that makes six bendings, the plan presents geometric complexities of constantly changing angles and directions. Trapezoids dissolve into squares and then expand to rectangular and triangular forms, yet there exist no awkward spaces, no strange, disfigured junctures. At every turn, dynamic, changing relationships stimulate a variety of spatial experiences. Roof gables angle in juxtaposition, making abstract patterns, and terrace shapes overlap and integrate.

To the left of the living room lies the two-story wing, composed of sleeping quarters and outdoor porches. As counterbalance to the two-story height, the dining room to the right of the central core stands 13 feet high, though the room itself is rather small. The effect, given the other dimensions, might

well have been of an outrageously out-of-scale box; in the hands of the Greenes it achieves bold spatiality. They divided the height into two distinct areas, paneling the lower half in white cedar and the upper area in redwood of darker tone, thus lessening the sense of a high vault overhead, while augmenting the feeling of intimacy. Visually, however, they brought the two areas into harmonious unity, suspending an elongated, vertical fixture of hexagonal shape that brings the ceiling into human focus.

The Pratt house is smaller than any of the Greenes' other major commissions, but the delicacy of handling and sensitivity of modeling make it as important an architectural statement. Though expensively finished in the interior, its small-scaled spaciousness and simple refinement of living areas could well be a model for a more sophisticated treatment of even very simple homes. Furnishings

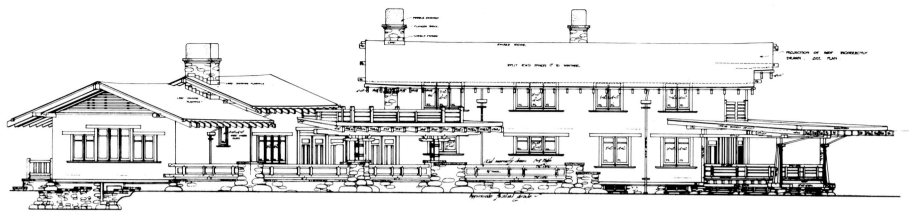

EAST ELEVATION

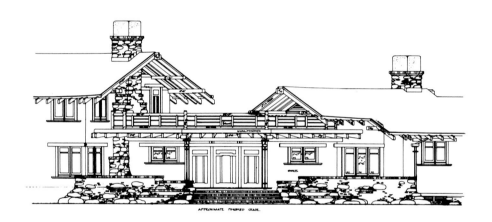

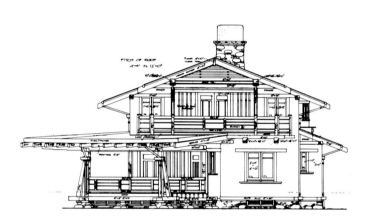

NORTH ELEVATION.

done by the Greenes are in keeping with the reduced scale of the house. They are exquisitely detailed pieces, particularly in the inlay work which revolves around pieces of jade and semi-precious stones.

In its placement within the site and use of materials sympathetic to the surroundings, the Pratt house stands as one of the finest and most pictur- esque houses in the best of the California bungalow tradition.

Following the completion of these four major residences in the wooden vernacular, Charles left for Europe for an extended stay. Within a few years, the brothers had built, furnished and landscaped the Blacker and Gamble houses, and had traveled to Berkeley and Ojai to supervise the Thorsen and Pratt houses; at the same time they had built several bungalows. No doubt they were both ready for a breathing space.

In 1911, after Charles' return, the firm received a commission from three maiden ladies, the Culbertson sisters, for whose brother, James Culberston, the Greenes had previously built a home. It was to be their last large commission and it poses many questions as to future directions the Greenes might have taken had circumstances and fate made it possible.

The Culbertson house represents a significant and bold departure for a firm that had built its reputation on the use of natural wood and whose houses were primarily known by their "woodiness," devoid as it is of all associations with the wooden vernacular. The exterior was covered with terra-cotta-colored gunite and, in the interior, there exists not a single piece of unpainted wood nor an exposed structural member, except in the flooring, laid in a herringbone pattern.

There are many known factors that may well have contributed to the choice of a new material, gunite. First, as one can clearly see from the plan, the shape of the site is awkward; what one cannot see is the steep, rocky hillside over which the site spreads. The Culbertson sisters, three fastidious ladies, required that all the rooms of the house be on a single level, but, at the same time, they did not want their bedrooms to be on the ground floor. This qualification, along with the nature of the site terrain, suggested extensive foundation supports. Second: "Materials suitable for building have not always been so varied in California as at present. Much has been recently added to the variety of home products," commented Charles, and a Los Angeles architect wrote, in 1911, that the use of reinforced concrete had grown by leaps and bounds in Southern California. The composite materials

Freeman A. Ford house, Pasadena, 1906.
(*House altered. Original malthoid roof removed and replaced with tile.*)
Above: *Batten door with wooden lock, original, adjustable fixture.*
Right: *Door with favrile glass panels in peacock theme carried throughout the house.*

Left: *Tichenor house, Long Beach, 1905. Detail showing timber half-frame with clinker brick fill.*
(*In altered condition.*)

Left: *James A. Culbertson residence, Pasadena, 1902. Front door of quarter-sawed oak with leaded art glass.* (*House remodeled by Greenes in 1906; later rebuilt and completely altered. Only original front door and oriel remain in exterior.*)

Above: *Robinson house; staircase newel post and railing.*

were overabundant, and the technology was then available to produce it. He predicted that very soon the permanent buildings in the area would be of the same light plaster as those found in places with a similar climate. A less easily proved influence may have been Charles' affection for Italian architecture, a love which might well have been rekindled by his recent stay in Europe.

Situated in the Oak Knoll section of Pasadena, directly across the street from the Blacker House, the Culbertson residence belies its large and expensive nature. With a low, unpretentious, cement-covered front, in material and form it could not stand in more striking contrast to the Blacker House. A seemingly modest, simple home, somewhat mission in appearance because of its tiled roof, it sits close to the front of the lot. But the house is a total surprise, for its excitement and unique character lie hidden behind the front facade and what appears to be a small and simple home reveals itself as a villa resting on a steeply-sloped hillside, landscaped into terraces and gardens like an Italian estate.

The Greenes used imagination and ingenuity in the placement of the Culbertson house to the site, capitalizing on the vistas the site offered, while statisfying the sisters' requirements. In plan, the house took on a modified U-shape that embraces a courtyard, a further adaptation of the patio plan. They faced one wing of the U to both the street and patio, and this wing, containing living and dining rooms, overlooks the vista of the Blacker estate with its beautifully landscaped grounds as well as the intimate and secluded inner court. The other, shorter wing comprised the sisters' bedroom suites; it lies at an obtuse angle to the base of the U, extending it beyond the edge of the slope. This placement elevates the bedrooms approximately 20 feet above ground and required foundation supports a full two-stories high, but the wing thus remains on nearly the same floor as the rest of the house. Taking advantage of the contour of the site, the front wing rests higher than the north, back wing so that an unobstructed view of the mountains lies before both like an Italian landscape. To the east, plaster sentinels support an arbor, visually completing the plan and the seclusion of the court.

Within, a gallery parallels two sides of the courtyard with a garden room angled from it. This room looks upon the enclosed court with its sunken fountain encircled with tiles of opalescent glaze and then to the mountains that rise above the oak tree tops of the grove below. Designed with a

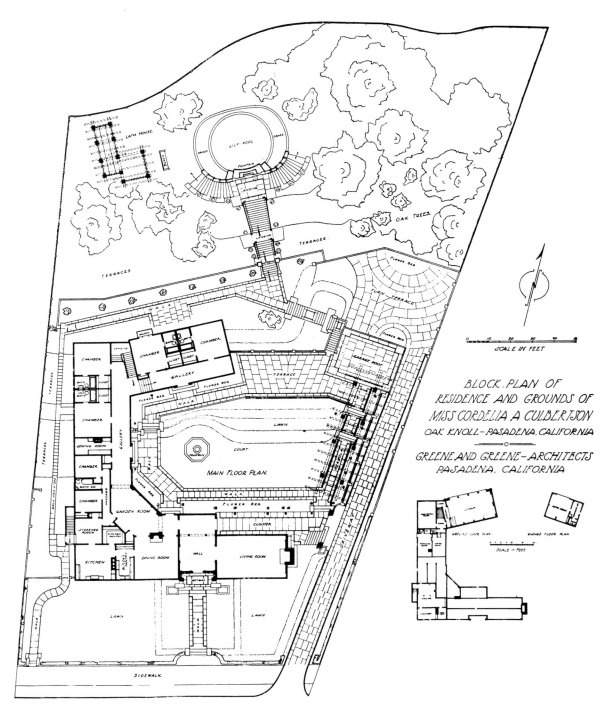

Residence for Miss Cordelia Culbertson, Pasadena, 1911. (Grounds subdivided; house presently intact with plaster exterior painted green.)

sliding glass wall, the sash was engineered to disappear into the ceiling and wire screens can be pulled down in its place.

To view the rear elevation of the Culbertson house is a quite different experience. Here the house unfolds itself, descending from the crest of the hill in ordered progressions of stair flights and tiers of dry wall. It encompasses the hillside as its own space, containing and molding it without violating the natural slope of the terrain, the whole surrounded by a gunite-covered wall. At the base of the hill stands a natural grove of live oak trees, shading stone benches and pathways that lead to a round lily-pool and a semicircular fountain.

The initial reaction upon seeing the interior of the Culbertson house is that it cannot be Greene & Greene. A closer look, however, reveals the same masterful hand, the same attention to detail, the delicacy of phrasing as unmistakable as Charles Greene's "Own True Mark." Light plastered walls cover the whole of the interior, tonally gradated from bottom to top, dark to light, in as many as nine different shades. They used wood, but painted it to match the walls, incising some of the pieces with geometric patterns that give an almost marble-like effect. The house expresses a plasticity of surface rather than structural expressionism of members. Coved patterns, like the profile of a lotus petal, melt wall into ceiling, and wave patterns, incised into plaster horizontal bandings near the ceiling, dissolve right-angled meetings. Continuous surfaces integrate each room to the others, and space—the cavity—rather than structure, seems to be the basis of form.

In this house, Charles blended designs, materials and furnishings from a rich variety of sources. He made a special trip to New York to buy for the house; some of the furniture he designed; other pieces were antiques. In concert, the furnishings exhibit a sophisticated, artistic blending of the finest designs and pieces from many periods and cultures.

In the entry hangs an antique alabaster lamp suspended on a silver chain from the vaulted ceiling. Other lighting fixtures, some of Greene design, contain no art glass and, in fact, no favrile or stained glass are used throughout the house. Charles designed the entry furniture with inlay in a twining wild rose pattern that complements the Bohemian carpet on which it rests. Living room furniture repeats flower patterns in inlay and Charles upholstered his pieces in the same silk brocade of black and gold that he chose for curtains and bandeaux.

Tones of silver and coral predominate in the dining room. Silver-toned velour covers the walls and the fireplace is composed of richly-variegated gray marble, accented by a centered panel of coral-colored Numidian marble. Charles incorporated the marble into the furniture he designed for the room. He inlaid the dining table with a rounded center-piece of marble; the serving tables and sideboard have matching Numidian marble tops.

Oriental rugs cover the floors of the gallery surrounding the court, and the walls pick up the tone in velour, acoustically quieting and visually adding dimension with their light-dark aspect ever-changing in the daylight. Brocade-draped windows illuminate the gallery by day, antique silver lanterns by night. The garden room is furnished with carved walnut pieces in the Queen Anne style, while the north-wing gallery contains wicker chairs cushioned with velveteen. Two of the bedrooms have lacquered pieces, one set decorated with painted roses.

In the Culbertson house, Charles at last found expression for his love of Italy's architecture. An outdoor loggia, Italian in both form and execution, lies under the north bedroom wing, accessible via a beautifully-engineered trapezoidal stairway of complex angles. One enters through a doorway of carved stone to this outdoor gallery that overlooks a terrace and the hillside, in true villa fashion. On the far wall, a marble reproduction of Michelangelo's "Madonna" bestows peaceful benediction. At night, Italian gilt lanterns, copied from antique design,

glow on the terrazzo.

The Culbertson house turned out to be an extravagant, expensive house and the Culbertson sisters, due to reduced circumstances, never had the opportunity to live in it. The Greene brothers completed the house for another owner, as the war years approached.

From the Blacker home to the Culbertson house, the firm's prime years, a subtle change had occurred, a change which, unfortunately, never reached full maturation, for the Culbertson's proved to be the firm's last large residential commission in Pasadena. Both houses were designed and decorated by the architects, but the Culbertson house portended a new confidence and maturity now that the brothers, both in their early 40s, had several hundred structures to their credit. In the Culbertson house, they not only used new materials with competence and originality, but they also employed familiar materials in different ways. In design, they seemed to have distilled the essences from eclectic styles, translating the Italianate to a form that fit California and its way of life. To furnish the interior, they drew from the richness of human experience and art—from the Chinese, Italian and English—blending the past and enriching their own concepts.

Less than 50 years had elapsed between the building of the first houses by the Indiana settlers in Pasadena and the Culbertson house. Two things were clear: first, Pasadena had accomplished her stated goal as a city of homes and a prime residential community; second, in the short space of two generations, Southern California possessed the talent and skills necessary to accomplish whatever its people aspired to. Almost everything that Greene & Greene designed could be made or fitted in Pasadena—the house itself, the furniture, even the art glass, composed in the Judson studios and the tiles made by Batchelder, editor of the *Arroyo Craftsman*. Everything was possible in this beneficient land and all things available for any life style to express itself.

The David R. Gamble House, Pasadena, 1908.
(State of best preservation in terms of completeness. Still has original furnishings. Given by Gamble family to University of Southern California and City of Pasadena, who presently maintain it.)

THE GAMBLE HOUSE

David Berry Gamble, son of one of the founders of Proctor and Gamble Company, decided, in 1907, to build a winter residence in Pasadena. Age 60, he and his wife had two children still at home, so the commission was for a family dwelling.

Today, as it did then, the Gamble house epitomizes the values that the residential style sought to express. It was conceived and designed to meet the needs of each member of a household as well as to foster a refined sense of values without pretention. Gracious without ostentation, large but not manorial, it was situated on a spacious piece of city property which the Greenes surrounded with landscaped gardens, informal yet carefully planned. In essence, it expresses the life style of properous family men of the 1900s who in their business-minded way sought a practical yet culturally refined place of residence. The Gamble house, too, remains not only one of the finest homes created by the Greene brothers, but also stands as a high-water mark of excellence for the wooden vernacular in America.

Totally designed and furnished by the architects, the David B. Gamble house endures as the most perfectly preserved of all with most of its furnishings intact. Because of that fortunate circumstance, it can be studied in detail as prototype, for in this home most of their innovative ideas and finest conceptions found fullest expression, and elements embodied in the Gamble House are found in adapted form in most of their major residences. Here, one can study the detail and gain an intimation of the whole of Greene & Greene. What follows is a visual tour of this particular home.

Apparently, David Gamble thought in similar terms to the Blackers, for he too chose to build a picturesque, unpretentious home for his rather large investment. Further, he selected the Greene brothers as his architects in a period when a retinue of prominent talented architects practiced in the Los Angeles area. The Gambles chose a site in Pasadena's west side, away from the stylish, rather formal homes of local society and, like the Blackers, they built a bungalow. Assuredly, it was a luxurious and gracious model, but it embodied the values that the bungalow sought to bring to architecture, and it served not only as a symbol of the fineness the bungalow could attain, but also as a model for lesser dwellings in the quest for the natural—sometimes copied with considerable success.

Clad in rustic materials, the exterior establishes a compatible relationship to the natural world with craggy shakes, stained to an olive green, and brown-stained structural members. Multiple roofs dominate the structure, projecting their parasol splines and seeming to have their own bases of support between the earth and sky. The house seems to breathe freely within the horizontal embrace of earth and roof.

Poised on the crest of a terraced lot, the Gamble house stands in an insulated setting that was architect-created, yet is within five or ten minutes' walking distance of the heart of Pasadena. The Greenes constructed a private street one block long, called Westmoreland Place, that parallels a main thoroughfare. They separated the streets, however, with a 30-foot wall of planted trees and shrubs and closed the north end of Westmoreland with high wrought-iron gates of their design, after construction of the Gamble House. Boulder gate posts demarcate the south end of entry, also Greene-designed, and thus Westmoreland Place is shielded from the dust of the main street and nearly disguised by natural barriers. Such an arrangement suggests an insightful approach to the automobile for, in 1908, the car was not yet the necessity it is today. The private street makes the residence accessible to main thoroughfares but eliminates traffic noise, which has increased greatly with the years. Six dwellings shoulder Westmoreland Place on the western edge, with their back to a bluff that drops 30 feet to the street below. To the west stands the relaxed pocket of "Little Switzerland" and, beyond that, the Arroyo Seco and the San Gabriel Mountains.

Placed nearly in the center of the parallelogram-shaped property, the Gamble House commands a magnificent view of the mountains. The land slopes away to the west and north, contoured by the architects, to enrich this rather dignified setting. Two eucalyptus trees, already growing on the lot, preside over the mound, and the roof was cut away in the back to accommodate their stature.

Cypress trees, planted in ordered progression along the front parkway, frame viewpoints of the house from the street. As one approaches, the house appears to be hovering over a sea of green, anchored only at one corner by the solid facade of a wall. In front of the house, the lawn rolls to a mound molded from scooped-out earth, and hides the bed of the semicircular driveway that rolls past the house. Laid in herringbone pattern, the bricks of the driveway crest slightly, becoming a transcendental symbol of the river and time, with the lawn sloping to meet it in protective banks. Secluded from view until one approaches, it curves quietly past the house as a stream bends to the shape of the land.

While the house, in fact, rests upon an extensive foundation of masonry and brick, this is invisible in an overall view. Surrounded by green plants and shrubs, the house seems to rise straight from the earth. Even the broad brick stairs assume nature's mantle of green, with hardy vines hugging and disguising the risers as though the steps, too, grew out of the land.

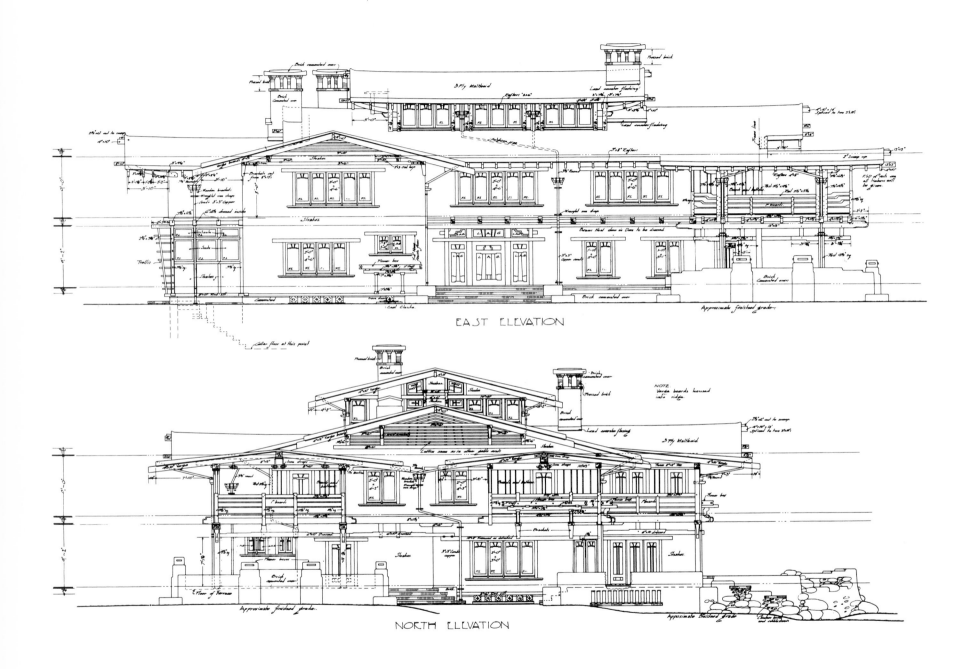

EAST ELEVATION

NORTH ELEVATION

David R. Gamble house.

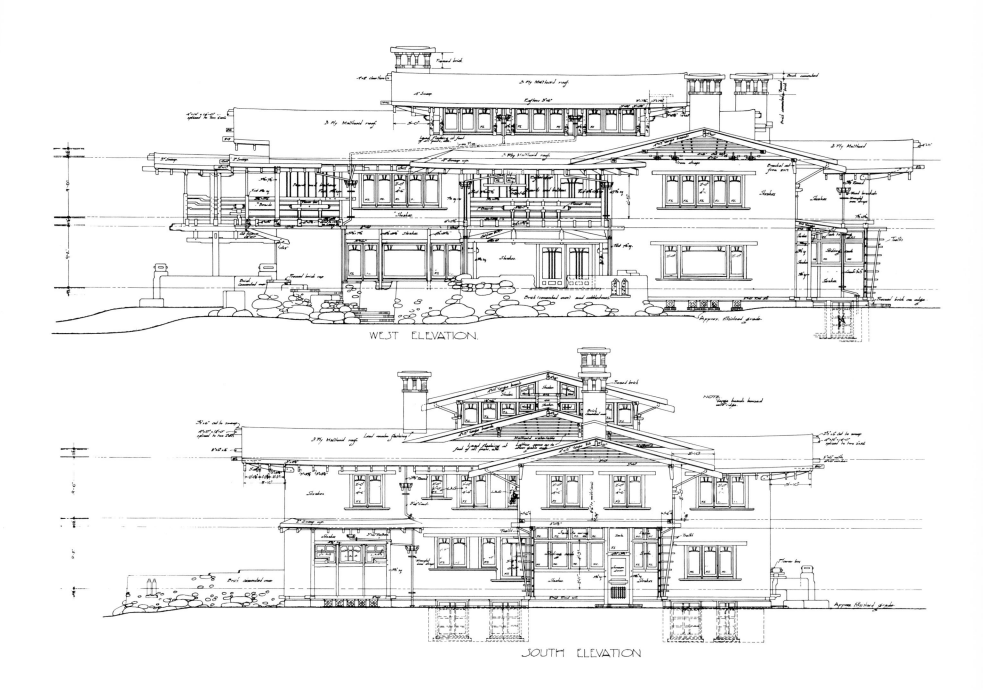

WEST ELEVATION.

SOUTH ELEVATION

71

The plan shaped itself around the lives of the Gambles evolving from their gracious sense of living that included both family activities and social gatherings. It was formed around people of position, yet was meant to be lived in and was a highly adaptable plan. It creates a setting of propriety for a gracious host to offer his guests pleasurable surroundings in which to share refined activities; at the same time, the plan provides a framework for each member of the family to engage in his or her interests simultaneously, while the domestic staff could quite literally disappear to do their work and serve when called upon. Family life in this house was planned for, both as a private experience as well as a communal one.

The nucleus of the plan is two geometric forms, with terraces and porches massed asymmetrically around them. The arrangement of the Gamble house constitutes one of the Greenes' most unique and subtle plans. A sizeable, rectangular hall is the major axis of the house, linking the front to the back. It separates the two geometries of the first floor: a rectangle on the left and a crucifix form on the right. The living areas, placed away from the street in Japanese fashion, all face terraces and each of these rooms is accessible from the outside. The total living space expands horizontally with the first-floor rooms opening widely to each other, yet with each spatial unit maintaining its own sovereignty. Thus the living areas are both integrated and, at the same time, articulated.

The crucifix form, enfolding living room and den, sits like an isle surrounded on three sides by a sea of terraces. The front terrace adjoining the veranda entrance is treated formally, sheltered by the canopy of the extending porch upstairs; the porch joining the den and living room is also covered to protect the outdoor entries. At the back of the house, away from the eyes of the street, the terrace spreads its tendrils in free, undulating forms, open to the rain and sun, with a small protected area, a shaded room-like space opening from the hall.

The rectangular form to the left of the hall axis encloses a guest bedroom, the kitchen and service areas, and the dining room, with its own small entry hall. This places the dining area apart from the main hall entry and extends it beyond the crucifix form. Entry to the dining room thus is disposed on a 45° axis to the living room, creating a seclusive, private atmosphere. In this position, the dining room sequesters a private opening to the terrace and a

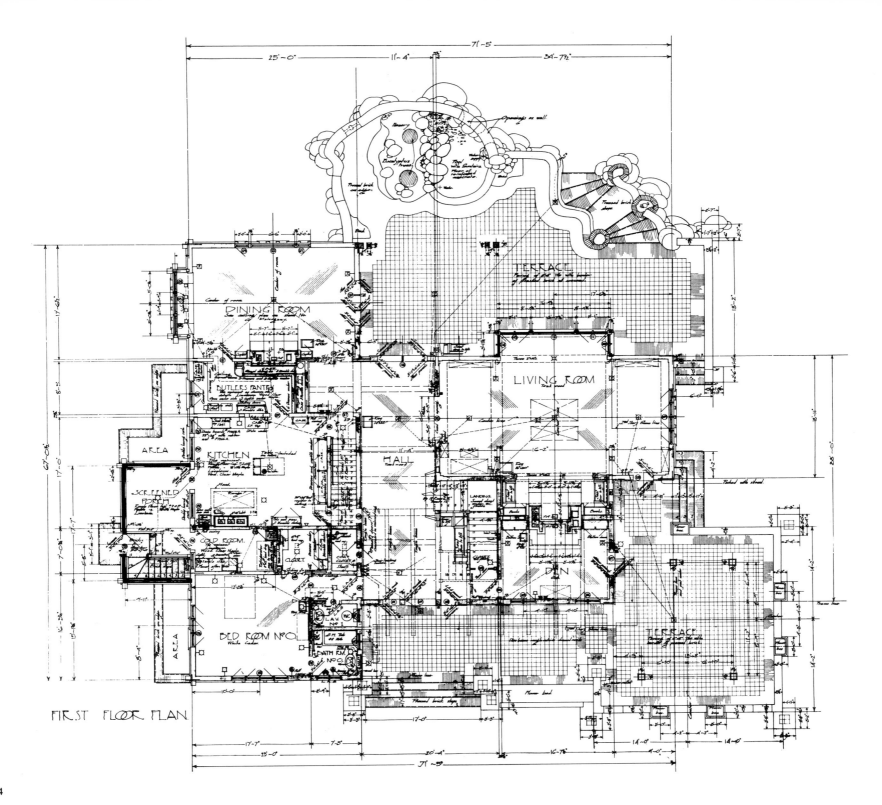

FIRST FLOOR PLAN.

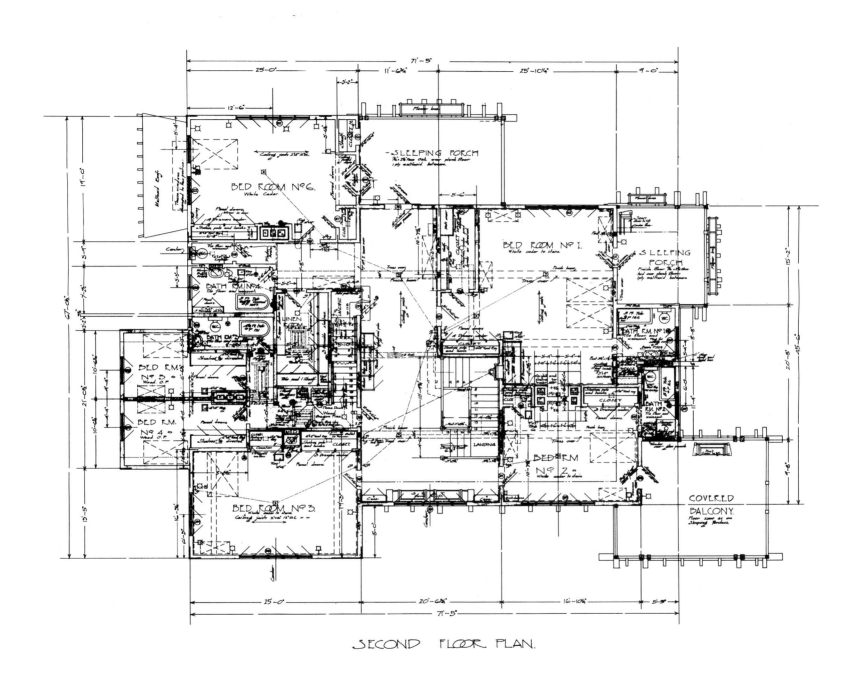

SECOND FLOOR PLAN.

David R. Gamble house.

view of the lily pool quite apart from the house—
another island experience.

In the frontal portion of the rectangle, a guest
bedroom with bath and a powder room is cloistered,
discretely accessible by a narrow hallway, left of
entry. To the right of entry, a quiet access to
Mr. Gamble's den, the tip of the crucifix, makes the
room a private affair where a guest would not
wander by mistake.

Recessed into the protective left arm of the
cruciform is the stairway to the second floor. In this
position, it leaves undisturbed the bisecting sweep
of the rectangular hall, which movement is repeated
on the second floor by a hall that reaches from the
front of the house to the back.

In the second-floor arrangement, the geometric
forms of the first are modified by porches that
reach beyond the first floor plan—open rooms that
penetrate and explode the geometries, extending
three of the four bedrooms. Under the canopy of
the wide-reaching roof, these outdoor rooms are an
integral part of the floor plan, not appendages to it.
In some cases they dramatize the sense of structure,
thrust as they are into space almost like cantilevered
forms. In others, the porches become voids, drawing
space into themselves and breaking up the mass.
Visibly, the porches are tied to the core of the house
by beams that project from interior to exterior, so
that the two elements create an interplay of forces,
the mass of the house projecting and receding. They
were finished like indoor rooms with the same attention to detail.

The entire second floor sustained the private
activities of the family. Two large bedroom suites
integrate many functions: each has a sitting area, a
fireplace, a space given to writing, a private bath,
and the outdoor room-complement for sitting or
sleeping. For one suite even the bathroom facilities
are separated, with the water closet located at the
end of a private hallway.

Two other bedrooms stand singularly at the
front of the house, secluded from the suites. The
largest outdoor room extends from the boys' bedroom and shelters the terrace below. Sleeping
quarters for the domestic help share the second floor
in nearly complete anonymity.

There is a single large room on the third level,
accessible by a stairway from the second-floor hall.
Termed "billiard room" for want of a better
designation (three billiard tables could easily fit
there, but Mr. Gamble apparently never played),
the room was necessary from the standpoint of

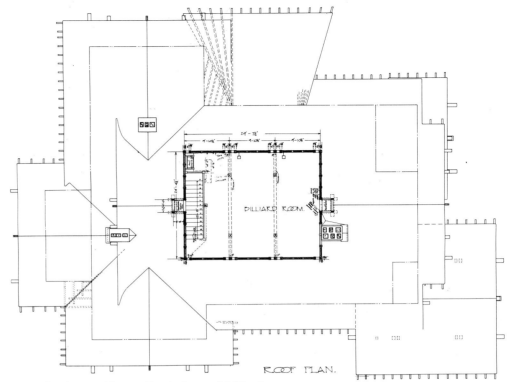

Gamble house. Above: *Roof plan and billiard room.*
Opposite: *Vine-covered risers of steps leading to front entry.*

design. It crowns the house architecturally, standing
like the pilot house of a Jules Verne space machine,
and commands the surroundings. Windows penetrate
all four walls, placing one above the outreaching
roof wings though in full control of the structure
below; it is a place for setting one's course and
sights. From here the house seems antigravitational,
capable of lifting itself from the horizontal embrace
of the land like a plane, wings readied for flight.
Practically, the third level ventilates the other two
stories, providing cross openings.

As in all of the major residences, the Greenes
kept the service areas out of sight; they remained a
separate domain which the domestic staff presided
over. Just as the servants remained distant from the
owner's personal life, neither did the family intrude
upon the personal lives of their staff nor the func-
tioning of the household. Situated in the center of
the first floor rectangle, the kitchen and attending
areas are enclosed with double doors, to seal the
kitchen smells and noise of preparation from the
house. A butler's pantry buffers the dining area from

the kitchen. Food is passed through a small window
to this pantry, spaciously equipped with dish closets,
and then served in the dining room. A standard,
separate service entry for all deliveries adjoins the
kitchen and servants' dining area.

Two stairways lead to the basement, one a
conventional back stairway for access to the laundry,
ironing, and vegetable storage rooms, and for service
people attending to coal storage and possible
plumbing or heating problems. The other stairwell
stands sequestered behind front hall paneling within
the service area, yet somewhat removed from it by
a second door so that Mr. Gamble had access to his
basement darkroom to pursue his hobby, photography. Another stairway to the second floor, secreted
directly behind the front hall paneling, leads to
the domestic sleeping quarters on the second floor,
so that servants, too, could disappear into their
private lives when the day's work was finished.

From the picturesque rusticity of the exterior
follows a quite different interior experience. The
broad entry door opens into an elongated hall,

Gamble house; front entry, depicting California live oak.

paneled in Burmese teak, that reaches the length of the house to the back terrace. Finished to a silken smoothness, the teakwood panels bathe the hall in golden tones when touched by the light from the open front door and the French doors at the opposite end. The feeling is of subdued elegance, of sensuous wood tempered by puritanical restraint.

Standing in the entry, the eye is immediately drawn to the stairway, nestled under the arm of the cruciform plan. Enfolding a bench within its U-shaped form, the stairway dominates attention with its endlessly fascinating details. Rectangular pegs reach out dimensionally, accentuating the horizontality of the stair planks, and small ebony pegs, placed in patterned progressions, add kinetic vitality. Joinery reaches architectural scale, imparting a sense of structural vigor as well as three-dimensional design. From the particular details that impart a sense of scale, tone and proportion, the whole begins to form and the beauty of the structural conception resolves any seeming complication.

From the stairway, the gnarled oak design in the entry, standing against an amber-gold background, comes to life. Spreading its boughs of stained glass to smaller doors on either side of the front door and to the art glass panels above, the favrile glass oak reveals itself as one homogeneous figure composed into a richly textured whole by the leading. Beautifully dripped and patterned, the metal banding gathers the colors of brown and green with slender and thick threads, sometimes smooth and then textured, into a vibrant symbolic tree of life. Such lead work, crafted in the local studio of Emil Lange, remains an extraordinary expression. Plaster areas of the hall have the color and texture of fresh biscuits, relating to the earthen tones of the art glass panels.

Corbelled stairs of the landing overhead recess the entry door to Mr. Gamble's den. From this secluded entry, the room seems to burst into height, with an oversized fireplace of reddish-brown brick coved into the ceiling in an arch. To bring the height in scale with the small-sized room, the ceiling was paneled and beamed in cedar, the possible heaviness of such treatment cast away by the upward illumination emanating from hanging copper fixtures. Built-in cabinets are of quarter-sawed oak. Many rules of architecture are violated with success in this room, for the overall affect is distinctly masculine and pleasing. A private terrace entrance provides isolation of use from the rest of the house.

79

Gamble house. Above: *Recessed fireplace nook with benches.*
Opposite: *View from main hall into living room.*

Gamble house, details.
Above: *Corner of living room.*
Right: *Corbelled and truss forms, done in teak.*
Opposite page, left: *Piano with case designed by C. S. Greene, sectional rug with tree of life pattern of Greene design.*
Right, above: *Fireplace mantel.*
Right, below: *Favrile glass lantern, fireplace inglenook.*

Gamble house; view from fireplace across to sunny alcove facing west veranda.

Close-up view, showing library table.

Gamble house.
Above: *Painted Rockwood tile in Greene-designed frame.*
Left: *Sliding door with opalescent glass panels that seals off dining room.*

Subtle changes occur from room to room, each giving forth slight variation in tone, feeling and aroma. Yet an overall continuity is emphasized by the exposed beams of the ceiling, varied in their criss-crossed patterns, which visually carry one from space to space. From the private masculine atmosphere of the den, the living room is quite a different experience. Rather than an entry door, the paneling seems to graciously give way to the room. Cruciform in shape within the larger crucifix plan, the living room is many rooms within a room. It is the residence of the muses, where places for music, literature, conversation and leisurely pastimes are provided. As a single, large room it can accommodate a sizeable gathering; used for separate entities, the living room allows for private, individual activities. The arms of the cross define two discrete spaces. One arm delineates a cosy, darkened inglenook, centered around a hearth with benches and bookcases, a private place to read or fire-gaze. The other arm looks to the sun and the land, extending

out to the terrace through windows on three sides. Like a conservatory, it provides a place for sunny musings and the contemplation of nature. The tip of the cruciform composes an area for conversation and the southern end of the room has spaces for reading and singing, with an upright piano clad in a Greene-designed case. Sectional carpets, designed by the architects and all of the same pattern and color motif demarcate these independent spaces.

Composed entirely in teak, the living room remains a matchless example of structural expression, where structure is not only felt, but is part of the design as well. Corbelled forms seem to strengthen corners and brackets appear to hold beams firmly in place. Metal straps which band members together lend apparent strength and artistic abstraction. Trusses delineate alcoves and become sculptural mediators between horizontals. Surfaces are subordinate to lines, which establish structural belief. Above a continuous horizontal banding which unifies the room space, carved red-

wood panels stand out in delicate relief. Birds drift among clouds and tree branches in lyrical counterpoint to the smooth panels beneath, divorcing the walls from the need to support the ceiling. Pegs bring members, together transcending flat planes, and end grain suggests volumetric solidity.

Incandescent lights, filtered through favrile glass fixtures, are suspended on leather straps. The darkest arm of the crucifix is illuminated with two lanterns of the same iridescent art glass. Natural forms waft through the room—clouds in bookcase glass, a sinuous vine creeping across the fireplace tiles, and the continuous flight of birds in the grain-rich panels.

Numerous pieces of movable furniture—rocking chairs, straight chairs and tables of various sizes—make it possible to create and recreate the room, according to the muse, adapting the cruciform to the scale of any function. Particularly unique is an octagon table, no doubt Ming-inspired, for the Chinese were adept in the use of the octagonal

Gamble house; entry hall looking toward dining room alcove.

form of which they were very fond. The backs of the rosewood straight chairs reach to a perforated crown, which climaxes the tall, curved back and suggests itself as a handle.

The dining room at the far reach of the rectangular side of the house is visible from only one corner of the living room. Double doors close the room and keep it from view, making dining and the preparations for it quite separate activities. The tonalities of the dining room radiate a sense of warmth and light, with every element luxuriously keyed to the silken reddish-brown of the San Domingo mahogany. Accents of crimson and green in the iridescent amber glass windows complement the Oriental carpets of burgundy which, in turn, accentuates and enlivens the wood. Floral patterns in carpet, glass and fireplace tile counterbalance the geometry of the room and relate to the natural world. Just beyond the row of windows in the dining room stands the undulant clinker-brick wall, surrounding the lily pond, with the mountains beyond.

Ashbee wrote of the Greenes' "magical" horizontal line, and nowhere is its power more eloquent than in the Gamble house dining room. A horizontal molding, moving in a continuous band around the room above door-height, scales the room to human dimension and creates continuity of line, gathering the advancing and receding planes of the room into a unified yet articulate space. It embraces the built-in furniture and encompasses the advancing hearth in a continuous sweep that prevents the complexity of parts from overwhelming the simplicity of the whole. Above the banding, a lighter-toned plaster area, nonbearing in aspect, lifts the ceiling from the walls and complements the browns of the wood. To illuminate the recessed sideboard, indirect lights conceal themselves behind amber favrile glass, giving a sunlit effect.

The dining room table stands on a single pedestal support. With cantilever supports under the top, it can be extended to double its length without separating the base. A cleated edge wraps the slightly curved contour of the table top, strengthened and graced by splines and pegs of ebony. The dining room table is simple in form and perfectly scaled both to the room and the human form, with no confusion of legs to detract from its simplicity. At the same time it possesses a remarkable elegance with its sensitively shaped, almost sculpted form, beautiful from every side. This single piece of furniture truly sets a standard of excellence in American furniture design.

Gamble house; dining room done in Honduras mahogany.

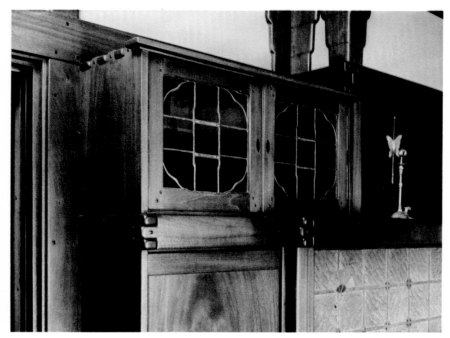

Gamble house, dining room details.
Left, above: *Cleated edge of dining-room table with ebony splines and pegs.* Below: *Pedestal support of table.*
Right, above: *Dish cabinet.* Below: *Wall lantern.*

Gamble house.
Left: *Coved brick fireplace carried out in quarter-sawed oak.*
Below: *Wall fixture in den.*

Opposite page: *Built-in buffet in dining room of Gamble house.*

To enter the stairway and traverse the stairs is an aesthetic experience. Structurally, the stairway touches man's innate, most primitive sense of form, with bold corbelled forms and sturdy posts. It is muscular and gymnastic in its bold zig-zag ascent and almost animal-like with its sensuously curved railing back, strengthened with splines. It challenges man's sense of art, for it is so composed and ordered that the whole becomes more than a sum of parts, more than the functional structure: stairway. Each of the three railing sections was carved from a single piece of teak, as the grain clearly reveals. Spatially, the stairway makes two directional changes with the first landing in view of the entry, the second landing facing the second-floor hallway.

Detail of stairway.

Opposite page: *Stairway of the Gamble house, done in Burmese teak.*

Gamble house, stairway details.
Opposite page: *View from first landing.*

Gamble house; second floor hallway, looking east.

Gamble house.
Above: *Window from master bedroom over stairwell.*
Right: *Stairway, looking west.*

Gamble house, master bedroom details.
Right: *Head board of single bed.*
Far right, above: *Bedroom chair back in walnut.*
Below: *Wall sconce and lantern.*
Below: *Fireplace in blue eggshell finish Rockwood tiles.*

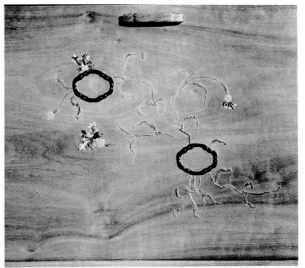

Left: *Letter desk in master bedroom.*
Above: *Inlay in drop front of desk.*

From the spacious axis of the hall, the bedrooms are detached in cellular units, each a private entity. The master bedroom suite is adjacent to the stairway. A thoughtful touch to this room is given by a pair of interior windows, in hues of blue art-glass, that open onto the hall. In the morning, as the sun streams through the band of hall windows, they selectively admit the morning light through two cloud-shaped peepholes, to give one a sense of the new day.

Conceived like the living room, the master bedroom enfolds the functions of many rooms within one space. It has a sense of entry in the form of a small foyer enclosed on either side by a built-in closet and wardrobe. At one end of the room, a fireplace of iridescent blue tiles provides a sitting area with a seat secreted away to the side. Another

corner is given to writing, with a desk of black walnut designed for the space. Charles interlaced the richly-grained drop front with a floral design done in fruitwood, ebony and semi-precious stones. Inside, he equipped the desk with assorted cubicles, two of which are covered with flowers of inlaid stones. The single beds were designed as a pair, each piece adorned with an asymmetrical inlay pattern that, in duo, make one complete design.

The bedroom has an outdoor complement, a room finished in batten-board with a built-in seat overlooking the terrace and the hills. Enclosed by railings made of rounded smooth members and joined with the same patterned pegs and dowels, the porch is an extension of living space, dissolving the sense of shelter as barrier.

The other bedroom suite is situated in the back

of the house with access to the same outdoor porch as the hallway. Comprised of many of the same elements, with Greene-designed furniture complemented by wicker, this complex has compartmentalized bathroom facilities enclosed behind opalescent glass doors with cloud configurations. Like most of their bathrooms, these rooms are painted in high-gloss white porcelain enamel and partially faced with white tiles. They are antiseptically sanitary in appearance in accordance with the new age of hygiene and contain Spartan commercial fixtures of white.

The children's room at the front of the house has the largest outdoor room. The placement of this grouping allows almost total privacy from the house, an important amenity for boys aged 14 and 18. The Greenes furnished this room in mission furniture.

99

Gamble house.
Above: *Wardrobe closets delineating entry alcove of master bedroom.*
Above, right: *Ceiling fixture designed to shed indirect, upward light.*
Right: *Linen press, second floor hallway.*

Gamble house.
Above: *Hall alcove; door conceals stairway to attic; leaded glass door at right leads to separate water closet.*
Right: *Detail of king post in attic.*

The attic stairway is enclosed behind a hall door and a panel containing a stained glass window with delicately tapered mullions. The attic, paneled in white cedar with rafter beams exposed, bares itself structurally, not only revealing but amplifying the sense of structure. Two king-post trusses seem to gather the thrust of the rafters and toss it upward to the roof, although in fact they are suspended, unconnected to it. A tenon joint appears to pierce the beam and be held firmly by rounded wooden dowels. Metal bands enfold beams, locked by wedges into secure supports. The structure of this room imparts vitality, a sense of bending and moving with the climate and atmosphere, yet strong and durable, ready to withstand nature's force. From here one sees the beams reaching from interior to exterior, the sense of structural soundness verified.

Gamble house.
Opposite page: *Bedroom in white cedar.*
Left, above: *Wall fixture.* **Below:** *Detail of mantel.*
Above: *Dressing table of white oak with mirrored image of room.*

Opposite page: *West terrace of Gamble house.*
Above: *Terrace lantern viewed from upstairs porch.*

The terraces surrounding the house not only expand the living spaces by forming and sheltering outdoor areas, they become the mediators between man and nature. Large flat areas reach out from the house in abstraction, sympathetic to man's step and psyche, then dissolve into the smaller geometries of brick that extend multidirectionally. Man's vision is contained, given focus by the wall that surrounds the back terrace, creating a sinuous delineation between them. Of clinker brick and rock, of man and nature, the wall varies in shape and form, embracing the irregularly-shaped lily pool. The geometry of the terrace changes direction and form, with bricks conforming to the rock and finally giving way to it. Finally, a lantern stands as focal point, poised on the wall. Man could set his sights by it and see the infinite, relate himself to the natural world, while knowing his scale and place within it. The lamp is his point of reference—in time, in place—and from a multitude of points, the object his eye inevitably focuses upon.

The Gamble house endures as the most complete embodiment of the principles by which Greene & Greene architecture may best be judged and known. It embodies the framework of constants —a rigid sense of integrity, a wide flexibility in execution—which took on myriad forms and phrasings.

Here structural expressionism, the essence of the Greenes' architecture, reaches for perfection. It forms the space and creates dynamic relationships as it brings structural members together. Articulation attains rare and beautiful forms, inspired by structural meanings, yet transcending them.

Wood is the primary substance, used as solid, plane and stick, and the stuff of their structural expressionism derives from the grace of adjustment of each part to every other—the kinetics of change when elements of difference are harmonized by elements of unity, the vitality of transition from one material or plane to another. Theirs is an architecture that expresses the nature of life, which is change, and they were able to orchestrate change—of tone, scale and direction, of material, connection and plane—with a vocabulary rich in variation. They are masters of the third element, the leaven that buffers the shock of change and attunes two elements to each other. They evolved a vocabulary of transitional phrases which are an endless source of interest in themselves and which together compose a sublime harmony. "Balance as a word expresses equilibrium of forces, but the word *harmony*

Opposite page: *Angled stairway from west terrace of Gamble house.*
Right: *Outside terrace entrance of Mr. Gamble's den.*
Below: *Construction detail of porch.*

implies far more than balance, which is merely mechanical reaction," wrote Charles Greene. "The idea of harmony embodies spirit, mysticism, emotion, reason, justice, consciousness, will, in addition to the first. Its action is coalescence, growth, metabolism."

Materials express their inherent qualities of design and beauty. They are brought together and coordinated by the principle of *notan,* where the value of one tone against another and intervals of tones create harmony of all elements. From the color of the room, the furnishings take their hue, toned to each other in varying intensities. Furniture complements the tones of the rugs and, in the main rooms, costly Oriental rugs set the standard for the color and motif of the other elements, touching every detail from fireplace to fixtures. In some rooms, rugs of muted colors integrate the values of the other designed or chosen materials in total harmony. It is as though they were constructing a painting, which Charles describes as a "repetition with variation of certain colors and combinations of lines in different parts of the same picture, so disposed as to lead the eye to some focal point. Every painter knows that any important color in his picture must be echoed in different places for harmony of the whole." The forms of fittings speak to the eyes, artistically and with cultivation—interpretation is superfluous. Despite the luxury, nothing offends, for everything speaks in muted good taste and the scale remains human and manageable.

Gamble house; lantern resting on wall of clinker bricks and cobblestones.

Irregular brick path delineating lily pond.

Gamble house.
Opposite page: *Doors of the auto barn.*
Right: *Meeting of the front steps and the circular driveway.*

It could be argued that the Gamble house was, in truth, a product created more in spite of the owner than for him, a product of the need for beauty and artistic expression on the part of the architects as much as the practical need of the Gambles for a home. It remains the artistic expression of man, its form derived, in part perhaps, from "aesthetic phantoms," without which, Nietzche said, "life would not be possible." So much that the Greenes created went far beyond the commission. One senses throughout that the architects provided the possibility of slipping away and escaping the mundane aspects of daily life or of turning around to gaze upon the exotic and fantastic. It fulfilled a need of the dreaming artist, but what of the client, for whom artistic visions were an unknowable entity? Drawings and notes from several houses reveal that the client, indeed, at some point halted the visions, for many designs were not carried to completion. In the Gamble house, a pergola reaching from house to garage never found form, and many furnishings were executed only on paper.

The dreams became folly, except to the dreamers, the architects, and in truth the house ultimately belonged to the architects. Greene & Greene sought to make an all-conclusive statement, to create a work of art. No obeisance was made to collections or displays of objects, no allowance for ostentation. It left the client and his expression behind. If there is fault to be found in the major residences that the architects Greene designed, it is that they can never be possessed, never really owned. They are never, truly, just a home.

111

Coastline south of Carmel, California.

EPILOGUE

Short-lived and intensely rich, the age of the Edwardians was drawing to a close. The realization that the old guard was changing and the romance of life fading, that things would never be the same, confronted the British side of the Atlantic in 1912 perhaps with more poignancy. Yet, omens on the opposite shore in those prewar years pointed to similar changes in American society. As the days of monarchies became numbered, with the attendant social upheaval it inevitably brought to Europe, the social fabric of American society also showed signs of fraying. The old values of gentility and propriety seemed stodgy and pompous, a bit too conservative as people rushed—now in automobiles instead of buggies—to seize fragments of happiness before they disintegrated.

In America, the signposts of a changing era were neither so disastrous nor so flamboyant as in the land of King Edward, but nevertheless they were there. While such indicators as art and architecture are rather less articulate or immediately noticeable in their reaction to societal trends, they are, nevertheless, fairly accurate reflectors of the social pattern. Architecture depends upon social organization for its existence; when social cohesion is lost, there is a stylistic decadence.

In 1912, the year of the Greene brothers' last major commission in Pasadena, the times did not augur well for architects who thought in terms of quality and custom work, where neither time nor expense was a major consideration. Their designs demanded a large entourage of skilled craftsmen. In the days when labor was cheap and material costs were twice those paid for labor, Greene & Greene labor costs inevitably exceeded those for material. The building industry was changing, economics playing no small part in modified building practices as costs rose significantly in the prewar years. The

necessity to economize on material, due to the ever-proclaimed shortages, became even more pressing. Large architectural offices, the trend since the 1890s, continued to grow, usurping the role of the individual architect and, at the same time, removing architecture further from the design of individual housing. The contractor-builder appeared on the scene, who could copy, at least in outward appearance, the work of such men as the Greenes and who offered it at a fraction of the price.

A house became an investment and people wanted something that showed the money, that looked, if possible, like more than the actual cost. The institution of the federal tax on income, in late 1913, only served to heighten the awareness that everything must be accountable dollar-wise. "Architects," wrote Charles Greene, "are pitted against a fast-prevailing economic contingent—the concentration of capital that seeks to control the entire field of building operation, combining real estate, building and investment." Labor became a commodity. How could craftsmanship, both time-consuming and costly, exist when competition demanded the lowest bid? And the artist, for all practical purposes, had to become a man of business ". . . transferred to the head of a department shared by engineers and foremen of construction and controlled by an efficiency expert," concluded Charles.

Within this aura, however, many wealthy clients existed, among them Mortimer Fleishhacker, a man of considerable influence in Northern California. He commissioned Charles Greene as his architect to build a country home just as the firm of Greene & Greene was completing its last residential commission. Just like the city dwellers of the East Coast who had summer homes in Newport, Rhode Island and Bar Harbor, Maine, it was becoming

fashionable for the socially prominent and well-to-do San Franciscans living in townhouses to have country retreats. On a rather less extravagant scale than the Edwardians who repaired to enormous country estates in that prewar twilight, many San Franciscans, nevertheless, built sizeable country houses, often verging on the ostentatious. Mortimer Fleishhacker, in his choice of Charles Greene as architect, commissioned a different brand of country home, one that was to be gracious but not pretentious, and refined without being stuffy.

Construction of the house began on the Fleishhacker site, in 1913. Located within a few hours of San Francisco, the house sits in a woodsy pocket on a 100-acre parcel of land between the coast and the inland redwood empire. In concept, the home had origins in the English country house tradition, which Charles, in his own inimitable fashion, transformed into an artistic and genteel summer retreat.

Green Gables bespeaks a gracious yet comfortable manner of living, but its particular beauty derives from its harmonious relationship with the land, always a special forte of Charles. Here, it is a sublime creation. Surrounded and enfolded by acres of rolling lawns, flower and rose gardens, an elm tree walk that melts into pastures, and the vistas of the woods, the house nestles into the terrain near the crest of a hill. The roof translates the slope of the hill and the clouds above into undulant, billowy patterns, shingled in irregular, wave-like rows. The profile suggests thatching, as does the light tan color of the shingling. The underlying roof line was shimmed to deliberately create a slight roll, suggesting earth and cloud in a climate known for its atmospheric changes. Charles covered the house exterior with gunite, the same material used on the Culbertson house, tinted to a rich earthen tone. Few exposed wooden members can be seen except for undereaves, joined by artistically molded brackets, and some articulated crux forms that grace and support the structure.

In massing, the house is disposed toward the extraordinary vista with a long wing, composed of the dining room, guest rooms and entry hall, opening to the veranda and expansive view. The veranda terminates at the living room, angled from the entry hall in full view of the landscape. A card room, juxtaposed to the living room stands in insular fashion from it, surrounded by greenery on three sides. The service wing extends from the dining area.

Charles carried out the entire two-story interior in tinted plaster, articulated and relieved by transitional touches that lend grace and dimension.

With Charles' imagination for landscaping given nearly 100 acres to roam, the Fleishhacker estate was to become a world of variety and beauty unto itself. From the back veranda embracing a large oak tree, spreads a vast sea of green lawn with two symmetrical brick paths leading to a lily pool that reflects the image of the house. From all parts of the house, the pool provides a focal point to view the vista beyond that seemingly ends in the clouds. Cast urns and richly-glazed ceramic pots of earthen colors punctuate the walks, the walls, and gardens— splotches of color with their blooming flowers. Over 200 ceramic pots of green glazed with blue designs were ordered for the grounds.

In a wooded pocket, away from the house, stands a dairy house to provide for the dairy needs of the home. Built of stone and settled near a small road, this structure seems ageless, a Rousseau archetype for the simple, good life. A small, square two-story building roofed in tile, it looks as though Nature bore it as one of her own. It is a poignant symbol of that yearned-for country life, close to the earth.

In 1924, Charles returned to the estate to furnish and decorate the card room. He designed a card table with four chairs and an armchair, and he carved three friezes, resting above the cornices around the room, and four cabinet doors. This is the only room in the house treated in the familiar Greene & Greene manner with displays of wood in natural colors. It is placed like an island apart from the rest of the house and can be reached through a small door from the living room that leads down two steps, or through an outside entrance. It is a warm mellow room in feeling, gathering its colors and patterns from nature, with the walls tinted in an earthy sepia tone to which everything else is gradated.

In the four-inch floor tiles are found the hues of field and forest which range from umber to sand-colored tan, dark green to pale olive. A bright yellow border of rectangular tiles, painted with a vine and leaf pattern, enlivens the muted tones as the sun does the earth. Flower designs, as though incised into wet plaster with a cookie-cutter, adorn the ceiling in a circular wreath and the furniture repeats the floral pattern. The tooled-leather table-top and the chair seats all possess a delicate flower chain. Charles carved a rounded oak tree, perhaps the large oak on the veranda, and the same flower petals found in the plaster, on the back of each chair in particularly bold relief. It is a simplified version of earlier work, yet intensely sure and powerful in form.

Each cabinet door and frieze depicts a separate scene, which together compose a global trek—each of the carvings on three cabinets characterizing a different continent. One shows a camel train traversing a desertlike terrain that typifies Africa; the second depicts the Orient with a landscape that is composed like a Chinese silk screen, and the third is of a chariot and driver, suggesting the Roman Empire of Europe. The last cabinet has a carving of a shipwreck scene on the high seas, with billowing clouds and birds swirling around the ship. Two of the above-window friezes carry out the global theme. One, nearly 14 feet in length, suggests a tropical paradise: streaming rays of sunlight fall on an island with palm trees, a thatch hut and natives. In antithesis, the frieze on the opposite wall portrays the Arctic. Penguins, dog sleds, igloos and figures clad in fur clothing populate the obviously icy scape. To complete his depiction of Planet Earth, Charles placed the seas on the third frieze, standing between the tropics and Arctic. Here sail three magnificent galleons on rolling waves, symbolic of the great ocean masses that separate the continents. Despite its relatively small scale, the 21 by 14-foot room enfolds a world of fantasy within its confines, with windows to the land on three sides.

Perhaps the particularly sublime quality of the estate derives in part from its protracted creation. Construction and landscaping continued over several years with both Nature and Mr. Greene contriving extraordinary natural settings. The *piece de resistance* of the estate and the architectural structure that climaxed Charles' career, is a Roman reflecting pool. It could well be considered the most fitting monument to remember this gentle, serious artist who worked and ultimately lived in a world of his own. Mr. Fleishhacker commissioned Charles in the late twenties to do a pool—what Charles Greene delivered was a body of water, 300-feet in length and 60-feet in width, that not only mirrored every fantasy of nature that surrounded it, but no doubt his dreamy visions as well. The Roman pool lay beyond the view of the house, below the edge of the land. It materializes as one stands beyond the lily pool, like an idyllic vision; it has the unreal quality of a Maxfield Parrish illustration. Charles Greene created a total setting to bring the idea of a reflecting pool to wholeness. He used a vast amount of masonry and various kinds of stones with the same sensitivity and truth to the essence of rock as to wood. Always the rock remains rock whether used for path, wall or arch. He terraced the hillside with tiers of serpentine-shaped retaining walls, laying the rock edgewise to reveal shape and substance. A retaining wall above the pool has a craggy specter, with rock edges silhouetted against the water below.

Elliptical forms terminate each end of the pool; at the far end stand open arches crowned by urn-like ceramic pots. These forms are composed of carefully-fitted stones that come together as a nearly flat, yet slightly dimpled, surface, like the watery reflections that mirror them. At the other end stands an enclosed grotto with niches, where plants and vines reach the water, a cool oasis. Fieldstones, chosen for shape and form, compose the wall, bold in pattern, yet smooth in facade. As the sun sets beyond the arches, it casts longer and longer reflections upon the water.

A swimming pool complex completed Charles' work at Green Gables. He placed it near the house yet out of view, building a set of wide brick steps to reach it, situated as it is at the crest of a knoll. The pool itself is secluded by a cypress hedge. Even here, Charles could not design the commonplace. He constructed a pool with two rectangular sides, the third stretching out in trapezoid fashion to accommodate stairs at the shallow end, and the fourth flowing out in an irregular, curving free-form. Two bathhouses, charming and simple, stand like sentinels on either side of the stairway, each capped with the same rolling roof as the house and built with the same careful detailing as every other structure he ever had a part in building.

·WEST·ELEVATION·

·SOVTH·ELEVATION·

·EAST·ELEVATION·BED·RM·WING·

·EAST·ELEVATION·

·NORTH·ELEV·

·SOVTH·ELEVATION·KITCHEN·
·WING·

Original presentation drawings of elevations for the D. L. James residence, begun prior to World War I, in Carmel, California. Building was protracted over several years, and the house was never finished.

115

Sea view of the James house, looking north.

View of the cliff site of the James house.

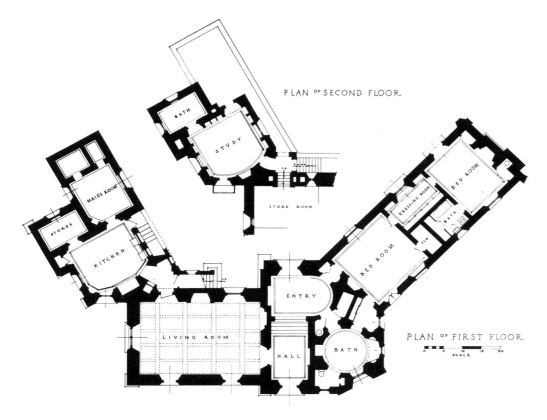

PLAN OF SECOND FLOOR

BATH

STUDY

STORE ROOM

MAIDS ROOM

STORES

KITCHEN

DRESSING ROOM

BATH

BED ROOM

CLO

ENTRY

BED ROOM

LIVING ROOM

HALL

BATH

PLAN OF FIRST FLOOR

SCALE

Above: *Plan of the James house as originally conceived by Charles S. Greene.*
Opposite page: *Gradated retaining walls rising from the cliff.*

Below: *James house; ceiling of living room with carved redwood beams.*

like a slop-shop coat; it will cover most any man's back but a gentleman's." Unfortunately, the supply of gentlemen previously described had retrenched to the past, seeking shelter in established styles; others of their rank felt it inauspicious to build with a war approaching and they pulled in their horns to watch and wait. And if, beyond that, the architectural climate were bad, Charles felt that the air quality in Pasadena was even worse (that in 1916). In the summer of that year, he packed his family off to Carmel. In his mind, the move was only a tentative one, perhaps the first stage of a final move further north in connection with the Fleishhacker involvement. But surely the brothers sensed, even if never voiced, that it meant the end of the firm of Greene & Greene. Perhaps the hesitance of the first step, with the possibility of return left open, eased the parting. Not until two years later did Charles inform the AIA in Los Angeles that he was resigning membership in that chapter because he definitely would not be returning to Southern California. Charles and Henry maintained their brotherly bond throughout their lives with visits and letters as they went their separate ways.

As mentioned, the building of Green Gables and the estate spanned several years, Charles traveling to the northern part of the state to supervise construction. He was no stranger to the area. Frequent trips had been made to oversee construction of the Thorsen house in Berkeley, and he and his family went camping nearly every year at the San Antonio Mission. This crumbling, forgotten home of the Franciscan padres lay on the northern part of the old mission trail that stretched between San Diego and San Francisco, and it was beloved by Charles.

By 1915, portents for the future of the residential style, as the Greenes knew it in Pasadena, seemed ominously clear. An article on bungalows, written by Charles that year, suggests the new attitude toward the residence; it was one that he could not work within. There seemed to be almost "a psychic affinity between the automobile mania and the bungalow bias," commented Charles, that reflected a last frantic hope to be free from convention: "Everybody is willing, even anxious, to try anything." Bungalow books, illustrating every manner of house, appeared, and the contractor-builder followed in their wake, ready to build whatever the client wanted, "when the training and better judgment of the architect should prevail," asserted Charles. "At no time has California been more active in the new and varied forms of so-called architectural production," but it was a debased and degenerate product, in Charles' judgment. As an architect, he maintained: "A house built to sell is

James house.
Opposite page: *Retaining wall with arch framing view of the sea.*
Below: *Side entry.*

Above: *Service entrance.*

Charles' last significant commission began before the war, was interrupted by it, then continued into the early twenties. Mr. and Mrs. D. L. James engaged Charles Greene to build a summer home which later became, as had Pasadena summer residences for many Easterners, a permanent dwelling. Mr. James was a man of literary inclinations, a collector of rare books, and his wife had artistic leanings. When Charles Greene showed them his idea, in the form of a quickly drawn sketch, of a house for their site, the commission was his. "Some of us" he wrote, "have our little dreams that come nearly true, paper castles that find embodiment." Charles' paper castle found real form in the James house, made of his dreams and memories. From the medieval ruins of Tintagel, standing on the Cornwall coast in England, which Charles had seen and sketched, to the humble Carmel mission, a few miles up the coast, he transformed them, the mighty and humble, into a vision of his own.

Fitting to the concept, the property looked like a remote, isolated kingdom, an estate populated only by evergreen and shrub and surrounded by an expansive sea of ever-changing moods. The jagged

121

Door to Charles Greene's Carmel studio, carved with peach trees in spheroid jars; begun in 1923.

rock mass upon which the house later established its foothold, had been hollowed by water and time, originally inhabited only by succulents and tenacious, hardy plants. Far below, the sea surges beneath the house and around it, and coves and sandy places remain secreted among the coastline. To the north of the site looms Point Lobos, a stretch of coastal land that has been made a state reserve of permanent wildness and beauty, perhaps better known as Robert Louis Stevenson's *Treasure Island*.

Born of the cliff from which it rises, the James house remains the most truly indigenous house of large proportion in the area. Built of rock, dynamited from the opposing cliff, its origins are in that rocky shore, its substance the same as the beaches of yellowish-gold granite. In other hands, these rocks have a generally unpleasant appearance, applied as they are, as flat surface and convincing neither as rock nor plane. With the sensitivity to material of the artist, rock appears as rock, becomes more than the thing itself. Charles cracked the rock and laid it in sheaves, edgewise, with the broken edge exposed. Crytalline substances that eons of geologic forces had formed reveal the inner life of the rock and the piled rocks conform to their innate character as building blocks. In the silvery light that invades the coast through shrouds of fog, the glow of the rocks brings the structure to life.

In essence, the house is a series of retaining walls and buttresses that emerge from the cliff as though part of the coarse strata of rock. The cliff face flows into man-made masonry of fine gradations assuming strong horizontal patterns that hark back to the primeval forms of such beauteous structures as Chaco Canyon. The sheaves clasp and wedge themselves into the rugged, irregular cliff, softening and molding its harsh outlines into spaces compatible to man. They terminate in low walls that delineate patios and verendas. These walls are capped with eroded rocks, taken from the beach, the same rock forms that Charles' friend, Edward Weston, photographed and made known to the art world. A fantastic amount of the total time and effort involved in building the James house went into these walls and buttresses, for they had to fulfill not only the requirements of foundation support but also artistic elegance. Charles entrusted the entire problem of masonry to an expert Scottish mason, who was assisted by only two other helpers and thus the building continued for years, for Charles delineated the property along the upper reaches as well with stone walls.

Charles Greene's studio, details.
Far left: *Bathroom door with story of Susanna and the Elders depicted in carving.*
Left: *Door in studio with Charles' note, "carv."*
Below: *Teak screen carved by Charles in the 30s.*

Entrance to the James property lies directly on the coast highway, marked only by an arch of stone that is part of the boundary wall and a wooden gate. From the busy highway, a narrow, winding pathway of stone leads to the serenity of the cliff site, where the house stands rather like a fortress, invaded only by the noise of gulls, sea lions and the crash of waves against land.

In plan, the house is comprised of two wings joined in a splayed V to stretch along the sides of the bluff. Such grouping faces every room to the sea. The house is covered with a roof of warm, reddish-brown tiles. Like mission tiles, these slightly irregular forms create an undulant line that makes the roof a fluid, rolling mass. Tower-like chimneys crown the single-storied structure, elevating it to a somewhat grand scale.

The stone forms and arches that compose the house are slightly reminiscent of mission architecture, yet again, transfigured by the guiding hand of a masterful architect. A suggestion of an arch appears in order to join corners and Charles placed an arch to frame the sea as seen from a window, to scale

the infinity of ocean to viewable proportion. Every door and window is arched—there are no straight lintels, for stone implies the arch as wood suggests the plane. Each opening has clear glass panes, framed in teak.

The living areas consist of one large baronial hall that opens to a patio through French doors, with a smaller room to one side. The kitchen area is to the left and a wing of bedrooms and bath to the right with access to the house through a circular entry. The rhythms and forms of the sea are echoed throughout the interior against a background of sand-colored plaster. Heavy wooden beams, carved with deep undulating patterns seem to have been gouged by the sea itself. Fireplaces of Italian marble warm every room, each carved with patterns of birds or sea life. They were a welcome and practical item in every room, due to the damp climate and availability of wood.

Charles made hundreds of sketches and drawings for the James House, becoming more and more involved as the construction continued over the years. Many changes were made as he went along,

his fertile imagination seeing richer and richer possibilities. Finally, the client called a halt. He was, understandably, quite unprepared to continue construction that seemed never-ending, for the incredible amount of time involved in masonry made progress painfully slow. In the meantime, costs continued to mount and shortages made some materials Charles had planned to use very dear. Mr. James requested that certain interior alterations be made so that he and his wife could move into the house and the interior remained largely unfinished. Furniture designed for the house was never built.

Years later the Jameses asked Charles to design bookcases for the study, the only room secluded from the main part of the house. It rests on the lower level and can be reached only from the outside via a narrow stone stairway. It is a charming hideaway, serpentine in shape complete with window seat and ocean view. It is a dreamed-of private place that busy lives could fashion as their ideal retreat. The bookcases, floor to ceiling, extend the length of the serpentine wall, installed after another world war intervened.

The James house was the last of Charles' Camelots to find embodiment. It stands today, secluded among trees grown up around it, one of the most beautifully constructed, organically-conceived structures on the coast.

Charles had built a simple frame cottage to house his family as soon as he had arrived in Carmel, with the thought it was only temporary. In a letter dated March, 1919, he wrote to the AIA requesting to continue his membership, but stating that he would not be permanently located for several years.

By the laying of the first bricks for his studio in 1923, perhaps Charles affirmed not only to his family but to himself that they would be settling permanently in Carmel. He and his sons had gathered bricks from the site of an old hotel recently torn down and had cleaned them by hand. Now they became the building blocks of his studio. It stood apart from the house and in that one large room, Charles Greene's intellectual, philosophical, and spiritual life expressed itself throughout the remainder of his long life. The building and decorating of the studio remained an ongoing project, changing as did Charles himself.

A small anteroom fronts the street, presenting the single-gabled facade of a small cottage. Charles used the found bricks, laying them in a Flemish bond, double wall pattern. Aging gives a mellow color effect of mottled red and white, with the thick and thin brick patterns adding dimension and a feeling of weather and time. To the left, an arched wall of the same brick remains only partially covered with tiles. A low arched doorway of solid teak is the entrance to the structure. Standing before this door, carved in low relief with twining tree forms that are laden with luscious peaches, is like finding at last that magic entry to the *Secret Garden* one imagined as a child.

The studio complex consists of one large, spacious room, illumined by a broad skylight in a low-pitched slope at the northern end of the room; the anteroom of entry, and a small bath and bedroom, all plastered in a soft terra-cotta color. A sinuous banding, impressed with plant and floral patterns melts the wall into ceiling. Alice Greene, Charles' daughter, helped him to carve the beams that reach across the ceiling. They exhibit the same sensuous sea rhythms as those in the James House, and to them Charles added other ocean forms—fish, crab, a maze of seaweed, and a bird—and interestingly, one Sufi symbol, an eye inscribed by a triangle.

Among the most personal and winsome of Charles' expressions is the small bathroom of his studio. In form, it is like the inside of a rock with no straight lines to be found. A narrow arch opens into a rounded shower stall that has just enough room in which to move comfortably. A precious-looking teakwood box with inset mirror hangs on the wall, serving as the medicine chest. Two arched doors open into the room and one feels that Charles decorated these purely for his own pleasure. On one door he carved the symbol he loved so well, a ship. On the other he depicted the Biblical story of Susanna and the Elders, where Susanna emerges from her bath as the elders, hidden behind the tree, look upon her.

In large measure, the furnishings of the studio reflect the inner life of this gentle man, for he gathered around him carefully chosen objects and personal things, thoughtfully creating his enviroment. Like a true artist, he was not a collector in the ordinary sense. Many of his things were not necessarily works of art nor was ownership an end in itself. Among his treasures were a grandfather clock and a porcelain bowl that had belonged to Benjamin Franklin, objects related to his New England heritage, for he was descended from such Revolutionary spirits as General Nathanael Greene and the famous abolitionist, Sumner Greene. On the parquetry floor lay several Oriental rugs, as they had in his architectural office, selected in concert with pieces of domestic Chinese furniture from the Ming period. Other furnishings included both Chinese cabinets and Japanese *tansu* chests, and there were things of his own design and making: cabinets and carved pieces and a rack for the coffee cups of his friends. He owned many Oriental objects such as bronzes, which had become for him a source of indefinable inspiration over the years. In a small niche above his fireplace, presided a statue of Jizo, a Japanese patron of children and a fitting deity for a man described as a "remarkable father." And there were rocks, bits of driftwood and shells—found objects of beauty that satisfied a longing and spoke perhaps only to the eyes of the beholder. In all, Charles Greene's studio was a very personal creation, simple and honest, with space to contain the growth and change that took place within. One can still read his note, "carv," on one of the doors.

Mechanism was taking command in the twenties and 20th-century man stood remote from that first being who forged for himself what Le Corbusier called "that indispensable and first tool"—a house. A by-product of the war had been the technical advancement of the gasoline engine and now, more than any other object, the automobile symbolized the dreams and values of that decade.

Both the Greene brothers had owned a car early in the 1900s for they found it extremely useful in their practice. But it held no other value than the practical, particularly to an aesthetic person, and Charles had lost what might have been one of the most important commissions of the day because of this. Earle C. Anthony, who had previously commissioned the firm to build both a home and a Packard agency, planned to build an extravagant Packard showroom. When Anthony saw his architect, Charles Greene, in a Hudson auto, the Greenes lost both commission and client who might well have set the firm up for years and put them in touch with a new clientele.

The car profoundly affected the American life style, reaching into nearly everyone's private, everyday existence. People focused on the automobile as the expression of status, taste and fantasy. The car assumed values far beyond the practical—it symbolized progress and that one was "going places." Getting there replaced being anywhere and speed became all important. People spoke in breathless tones of "fast cars," the "fast crowd," and "fast women." If a man was no longer master of his

View of Green Gables, Fleishhacker country home,
mirrored in lily pool; Woodside, California, 1912.
(Home still maintained by original family as a summer residence.
It is unaltered and in an excellent state of preservation.)

Right: *Dairy house, Fleishhacker estate.*

house, he could at least sit behind the wheel of his machine and feel himself master of his environment and his fate.

War had brought inevitable change; life patterns never regained the savor or substance of the good old days. The twenties were hardly an age of subtlety—nothing succeeded quite like financial success and sophistication, a fast wit and studied lack of seriousness toward life were cultivated values.

The social order upon which the residential style based its standards retrenched to stock-broker Georgian, buying authentic antiques and period pieces, believing that security and values could be attained by investing in another period and style. The new social set, those made wealthy by the war, had no association with old society and

quickly broke the hold of those whom they considered "seedy types." With their naive and uninitiated tastes, they attempted to surround themselves with tradition. They called upon the architectural profession to build suitable homes in which to display their wealth and, naturally, architects provided them with the correctness of Beaux Arts classicism, whatever their own proclivities may have been. As Charles commented, "I am forced to admit that as creatures of environment, few of us are able to thwart the thrust of immediate pressure." Employing the best decorating firms to swathe them with symbols of their class, the newly-rich were engulfed in splendor as these companies readily responded with lavish period schemes and trappings that looked (and were) expensive and ostentatious.

Fleishhacker estate. Above: *arched colonnade opposite the grotto, terminating the reflecting pool.*
Opposite page: *Roman reflecting pool.*

Even if there had been a clientele for the Greenes, building practices had changed drastically along with everything else. Generally, machine standardization created a uniformity of materials, and new technological discoveries such as the bonding of wood and metal, brought into being such materials as plywood. The war-time emphasis upon economy in both material and labor, became the post-war norm of generally lessened quality. Skilled craftsmen had been siphoned to other luxury trades, such as automobile body shops, where they formed car bodies entirely in wood. Airplane manu-

facture, spurred by the war, boomed and craftsmen turned their talents to such well-paid industry.

The machine had never appealed to Charles, but that would have been a surmountable obstacle had he wished to continue in practice. No doubt he could have been in the forefront, utilizing the latest and most efficient means and materials. But the square, uniform world that mechanism created was anathema to his nature and, in his mind, to architecture as well. "The insidious machine, from year to year has driven from the masses personal expression by art process." Many, however, were

absorbed with the machine as the new wave of art, and the Exhibition of the Decorative and Industrial Arts in Paris, in 1925, reflected the beginnings of "modernism" and the anti-decorative trend. Le Corbusier looked to a more impersonal art and termed architecture a "machine to live in." For him, the clean lines of the ocean liner were a source of inspiration, and Frank Lloyd Wright looked to the machine process to carry out his architectural perceptions. Charles Greene turned his search for art inward, becoming more introspective, and more deeply involved in his philosophical studies.

Henry Greene, more adept than his brother in practical business ways, remained in Pasadena and continued the architectural practice under the firm's name. He built several houses, one a sizeable residence in Hollywood, and another for one of Pasadena's mayors, but nothing on the scale of the firm's previous work. Charles, sustained in part by an ongoing relationship with Mortimer Fleishhacker, whose various commissions continued over a period of years, worked in his own quiet way, true to his nature and his talent. He had written, in 1918, a prognosis for the revival of the art process in building, concluding that "the architect must not be too hopeful of the immediate outcome. His position may long continue to be humble and his fortitude will, without doubt, be tried to the utmost. As for his ideal, it must be imperishable." And so it was, and Charles withdrew to wait. He removed himself from the "chaos of unrestrained commercialism" and trying to construct within the "haste of speculation," but he continued to build, if the opportunity presented itself. He designed a music studio in Piedmont, California, for his very close friend, Robert Tolmie, and he was called on to do many alterations and additions for various clients over the years.

As the depression years descended, paralyzing the country's activity, business came to a standstill for nearly every architect. Henry Greene closed his Pasadena office and moved the business to his home, and other architectural offices dropped from sight.

In Charles Greene's life, the depression had little effect and the thirties were very good years. He continued to make some furniture from time to time and to do much carving and sketching, but his artistic spirit had found other outlets. His studio became a center of activity, open for concerts, lectures and friends. Charles found a small community of free spirits with whom he could share his thoughts on art, beauty, and truth—Edward Weston, one of the first photographers to be known and respected by artists; Gustav Eckstein, a writer, and his wife, Francesca Behdiha, a violinist with whom Charles' youngest daughter studied; and the musician, Robert Tolmie, a prominent teacher and pianist from the Bay Area.

In the early '30s, Charles and his wife, Alice, had become involved with a study group deeply interested in the teachings of Gurdjieff. All his life, relates his youngest daughter, he had been interested in various philosophies, and the involvement with

this group meeting regularly to discuss the teachings lasted for several years. During these years he wrote a good deal, expressing himself on a variety of subjects, particularly art and philosophy, as well as writing a novel about a young architect, about which one only can conjecture that much was autobiographical.

Charles had his eccentricities. He considered himself a frail man though he lived to an old age, and he was concerned quite early about natural food and the adulterants added to it; his wife ground wheat in a hand mill with which to make his bread. A daughter remembers, "He could be quite testy with familial things . . .. It would take 'years' for him to write a cheque, but when he was finished it was a work of art, each letter and figure would be so beautifully printed."

As the years progressed, the spiritual aspects of life engrossed more and more of his being. He had been fascinated with the Orient from the earliest days. It had begun as a decorative interest, went on to the structural and, in the late thirties, evolved to the philosophical. Charles became deeply involved in Buddhism, which, said a daughter, "eventually made him relinquish everything else. He practiced for many years . . . withdrew more and more from daily life as time went on." He had daily meditation periods and like the New England transcendentalists, sought to rise beyond the duality of life.

In the late '40s, articles began to appear in Sunday magazine supplements, reviving interest in the work of Greene & Greene, now more than three decades old. As an art form, mechanism fell into disrepute, the proponents of the machine seeming to be false prophets. Where the machine had originally been a simulation of man's physical body, an intimate extension of man's power, it now seemed to dictate to him what was to be made in mass numbers. Such giant megamachines as the *Queen Mary* were, in fact, the last heralds of the mechanical age where manned levers and gears still predominated. For one such as Charles Greene, who believed "buildings after all are only an extension of man's wardrobe . . . quite personal in their appeal," the disillusionment had been early. Now the renewed interest in the Greene brothers came hand in hand with the humanism some people sought to restore after another more devastating war had taken its toll. In 1948, the Southern California chapter of the AIA bestowed a Special Certificate of Merit upon the brothers, and the AIA followed with a citation in 1952.

Enthusiastic articles by people such as Jean Murray Bangs sought to draw attention to the Greene's work, pointing out certain features of their homes that seemed modern and their approach to solving architectural problems as avant-garde. Others exploited their work as being part of the American heritage of quality craft and still others sought to revive the lumber trade by pointing out the brothers' use of California woods.

Clay Lancaster discovered the Greenes as he traced the thread of the Japanese influence in America. He interviewed each of them in 1954, both men then in their '80s. Henry Greene was able to relay many factual pieces of information to Mr. Lancaster about architectural practice. He remembered the people who had helped build many of their commissions and the firms which had made custom furnishings to their designs. He expressed a deep sense of pride over the recognition accorded to them by the AIA. When Mr. Lancaster saw Charles Greene in his studio, he was a very sweet, gentle man with thin, silky white hair falling nearly to his shoulders. He showed his interviewer mounds of photographs and drawings—of Japanese buildings, of the firm's, of his own. The factual details of their work were no longer of interest to him, but the spirit of it was still alive within him as he sat in the sanctuary of his studio.

His days of building had long passed and perhaps the age of wood as well. But sitting in his favorite chair, rubbing the wooden arm as his family had seen him do on countless occasions, it didn't matter. "There is in wood," he had once written, "something that stimulates the imagination, its petalous sheen, sinuous grain, delicate shading that age may give to even the commonest kind of wood."

Henry Greene died before his elder brother, in 1954, and Charles died three years later. For such a brief period, really, in their long lives had they been allowed to produce their art. One wonders what more they might have done had time, circumstance, fate . . . but Charles would only have replied:

Energy of the Architect floweth as the river
Whether men want it or turn it into a ditch
  bideth not with him . . . .
But for a gleam of beauty he dieth and liveth
  again.